East of Malta

West of Suez

THE ADMIRALTY ACCOUNT OF THE NAVAL WAR IN THE
EASTERN MEDITERRANEAN: SEPTEMBER 1939 to MARCH 1941

THE ITALIAN CHALLENGE. This Italian propaganda
cornered and helpless in the face of Italian sea and air p

of June, 1940, represents the British and French Fleets
Against these odds the British Fleet was to fight alone.

THE FIGHT BEGINS. The gunners grimly wait for the next attack.
Smoke pours up from a shattered and disintegrated Italian torpedo-bomber.

EAST OF MALTA
WEST OF SUEZ

The Admiralty Account of the Naval War
in the Eastern Mediterranean
September 1939 to March 1941

PREPARED FOR THE ADMIRALTY
BY THE MINISTRY OF INFORMATION

London: His Majesty's Stationery Office

CONTENTS

Price 1s. od. *net* from His Majesty's Stationery Office at York House, Kingsway, London, W.C.2; 120, George St.,
Edinburgh, 2 ; 39-41, King St., Manchester, 2 ; 1, St. Andrew's Crescent, Cardiff ; 80, Chichester St., Belfast ; or
any bookseller. Printed by The Amalgamated Press, Ltd. (Printing Works), London, S.E.1. S.O. Code No. 70-413*

THE FIRST ATTACKS. The British Navy takes the initiative as H.M.S. Dainty destroys three Italian submarines off Crete in one day: June, 1940.

THE APPROACH TO TARANTO. The Illustrious and her destroyer screen part company with the 3rd Cruiser Squadron: 11th November, 1940.

ON THE ARMY'S FLANK. The monitor Terror and the gunboats Ladybird and Aphis bombard Italian bases in Libya: December, 1940.

SKIRMISH BEFORE MATAPAN. The cruisers Orion, Ajax, Perth and Gloucester draw the enemy towards the Battle Fleet: 27th March, 1941.

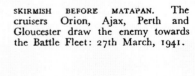

The paintings reproduced here are by Lieut.-Cdr. Rowland Langmaid, R.N., who was attached to Admiral Cunningham's staff as official Admiralty artist. Acknowledgement is also due to Lieut.-Cdr. G. M. S. Stitt, R.N., on whose sketch-maps four of the maps included in this book are based.

This book describes the work of the British Navy in the Eastern Mediterranean from the outbreak of war until the spring of 1941, by which time British supremacy in these waters had been vigorously asserted at Taranto and Matapan. This is a naval story, but to understand its full significance it is necessary to look beyond the narrow seas in which it was enacted; for the part played by the Navy in the Mediterranean has an importance in world strategy which it would be difficult to exaggerate. If during these eighteen months the British Navy had not been successful in maintaining its control of the eastern basin against greatly superior enemy forces, Malta, Suez and Alexandria might all have fallen, the campaigns in Abyssinia and Syria would hardly have been possible, our whole Middle Eastern position would have been endangered and the Axis might have reached the Indian Ocean from the west. Such was the Navy's achievement in the Mediterranean in 1940–41.

1. The Narrow Seas

SOMEWHERE OR OTHER there is of course a land background to all sea warfare; its shape governs to a large extent the strategy of fleets. But apart from this geographical outline, the land has three distinct and vital qualities in the eyes of seamen: it is hostile, or benevolent, or neutral; and in this neutrality there are sometimes tendencies either way.

In some theatres of war what goes on ashore may be so far away that the seaman does not see it as his immediate concern. He carries on with his job, escorting convoys, mine-sweeping, submarine hunting, or whatever it may be, indifferent to the clash and sway of armies. In narrow seas, however, land and sea warfare are in perpetual reaction to each other; a bayonet charge may pass a convoy through a danger area unscathed; a sortie of British cruisers help to turn a German tank retreat into a rout.

Over it all swoop the bombers and the fighters, keeping the fortunes of the opposing forces in continuous oscillation.

In peace time the Mediterranean meant little more to Britain than a 1,900 mile seaway, a vital passage to and from the Suez Canal and the East. It was the Navy's task in war to guard this sea road, to maintain the heritage of sea power in the Mediterranean bequeathed to it by Nelson. The Fleet had three bases: Gibraltar at the western entrance, Alexandria at the eastern end, Malta

roughly halfway between the two, sixty miles, as the bomber flies, from Sicily.

On the declaration of war the entire Mediterranean coastline was either Allied or neutral, with the exception of the strip of British-mandated Palestine, with an oil pipe-line to Haifa.

The neutrality of Spain, exhausted by civil war, was unsympathetic. Our alliance with France gave the Fleet harbourage in the west at Toulon, and guaranteed the security of the other fork of the oil pipe-line from Iraq,

"IT LOOKED PRETTY GOOD." When war began, the entire Mediterranean coast was Allied or neutral, and the British and French Fleets ruled the sea unchallenged. Allied coastline is shown light, neutral coastline striped.

EVE OF BATTLE, MAY, 1940. The Eastern Mediterranean Fleet, reinforced by a powerful French squadron, lies at Alexandria ready for action. At midnight on 10th June Italy declared war.

which ran to the sea through Syria, a French mandate.

Italy's previous attitude suggested that her neutrality was not of great stability, but she was not actively hostile. Yugoslavia, Greece and Turkey, glancing apprehensively to the north-west, were well-wishing and watchful.

Egypt was also neutral. Under the terms of the Egyptian Treaty of Friendship we had the use of Alexandria as a naval base and port of maintenance for the Fleet. It suited her to refrain from a declaration of war on Germany, but she severed diplomatic relations with the enemy and declared an *état de siège*, inviting our help in the protection of the Suez Canal Zone, which is under her suzerainty.

From the Egyptian frontier the Libyan desert stretched westward for nearly five hundred miles, a not very lustrous jewel in the Italian Empire's crown. Its main port was Tripoli, away in the west. A motor

road, constructed with immense labour by Italian engineers, skirted the coast, linking a few insignificant harbours whose names— Bardia, Tobruk, Derna, Benghazi—meant very little to anybody. To the west lay the French naval bases at Bizerta, Algiers and Oran.

This, then, was the background of the arena in which the British Fleet was destined to fight for its heritage against longer odds than ever before in its history. And on the face of things, as it appeared to the Navy then, that background looked pretty good.

The man holding the responsibility of the Mediterranean Fleet Command at the outbreak of war was Admiral Sir Andrew Cunningham. He had fought the last war in command of a destroyer in the Mediterranean; and when, seventeen years later, he reappeared in the same narrow seas as the Rear-Admiral of the destroyer flotillas, the name of his first command, the Scorpion,

his balcony to excited mobs and founding his African Empire with gas and bombs and the expatriation of bewildered peasants. The Rear-Admiral commanding the destroyers, holding his flotillas in leash at Alexandria, had the measure of it all.

He left the Mediterranean in 1936, to return the following year as Second in Command of the Mediterranean Fleet, with his flag flying in the Hood. It was as if destiny had selected him to be forever helping to sharpen the weapon that was to hold the narrow seas. A brief spell at the Admiralty as Deputy Chief of the Naval Staff followed, while the skies darkened over Europe, and in June 1939 he returned to Malta to command the Fleet.

2. The Quiet Before the Storm

was still a legend. During those years he had been Captain of the battleship Rodney, and Commodore of the Royal Naval Barracks at Chatham, but most of his time had been spent in active command of destroyers, or in administration of a destroyer base.

His knowledge of destroyers, of what they were capable, of their tactics in narrow seas in war, was unique. He acquired it in a grim school which required the power of instantaneous decision, of grabbing at the essential lever in an emergency when every second counted; and in spite of having commanded one of the two largest battleships afloat, he never quite lost the old destroyer captain's instinctive disdain for the might of the capital ship. Destroyers nearly always fight against odds, and this attitude becomes inbred in the minds of the men who handle them.

While Admiral Cunningham was the Rear-Admiral of the destroyer flotillas in the Mediterranean, Mussolini was baying from

ON THE DECLARATION of war, the security of Egypt and the Suez Canal governed naval strategy in the Mediterranean. Our French allies immediately assumed responsibility for the western basin, between Malta and Gibraltar; a British destroyer force guarded the Straits of Gibraltar; the main fleet lay at Alexandria cleared for action, waiting for Italy to declare her hand. Shipping through the Mediterranean came to a standstill, but not a movement of warships took place that could be construed as the trailing of the Fleet's coat-tails past Italy's doorstep.

The tension gradually relaxed when Italy

announced a policy of non-belligerency. She went further, limiting the areas in which her submarines patrolled, and making no fleet movements.

Trade through the Mediterranean was resumed, shipping being run in convoys escorted by destroyers to guard them against the possible presence of German submarines.

The Navy, exercising the ancient right of a belligerent of " visit and search," commenced a patrol of the Aegean, the approaches to the Adriatic and the waters to the south of the Straits of Messina. Ships suspected of carrying cargoes destined for Germany were taken for examination to Port Said, Haifa or Malta, where contraband control bases were established. Nothing could pass by Port Said or Gibraltar without rigid control. Not a shot had been fired, but sea power had effectively throttled enemy supply lines through the Mediterranean.

Cruisers, a few armed merchant-cruisers and boarding vessels, sufficed for the task. The Battle Fleet, as long as Mussolini behaved himself, could be sent westward through the Straits of Gibraltar to reinforce the Fleet in home waters. In the brief lull afforded by Italian neutrality and French alliance, convoys were abandoned ; the expected German submarine menace did not materialise, and merchant shipping proceeded without escort. In November, 1939, the Commander-in-Chief, deprived of his fleet, hoisted his flag ashore at Malta.

A period of comparative tranquillity in the Mediterranean followed. It was made the most of by the Allied navies, whose Admirals and staffs met in frequent conferences at Malta and Bizerta to evolve plans for concerted operations in the future. The *bon accord* of these allied meetings and the mutual trust that bound seamen who had fought together against Germany in the last war seemed to be unassailable.

The Commander-in-Chief paid visits to the Army and Air Commands in Cairo and conferred with them and the French Command in Syria. The small army in the Middle East was reinforced by Australian and New Zealand divisions who went into training in Palestine, while a steady unobtrusive reinforcement of the Italian army in Africa flowed into Tripoli. But just then the threat of an attack on Egypt across the waterless Libyan desert did not seem very serious.

Early in 1940, Italian neutrality deteriorated into passive hostility towards the Allies. By the end of March, 1940, she had made it plain that she was only biding her moment to throw in her lot with Germany. The lull was nearly over and the gathering storm sent the Battle Fleet back from home waters to the Mediterranean, and reinforced it with cruisers from the East Indies, the aircraft-carrier Eagle and some submarines from China. The Commander-in-Chief hoisted his flag afloat and led the Fleet to Alexandria.

It was now May. A French squadron of three battleships, four cruisers and some destroyers joined him from the western Mediterranean. A month was still available in which to weld the collection of ships of two nations and all classes, strangers to each other from all over the world, into a fighting fleet. It gave time for the shore and maintenance services at Alexandria to be placed again on a war footing, and the final plans for co-operation made with the sister services in the Middle East.

France was now fighting for her life against the German mechanised onslaught. The Mediterranean had been closed as a supply route from the United Kingdom; reinforcements must take two or three months to reach Egypt by the Cape and Red Sea route. Italian military and air force concentrations in Africa far outnumbered ours. Malta seemed an easy prize. Mussolini looked at it all and decided the moment had come. It must have appeared to him, to use a naval colloquialism, like " money for old rope." At midnight on 10th June, Italy declared war against France and Britain.

ADMIRAL CUNNINGHAM took the Battle Fleet to sea on 11th June, the day after the Italian declaration of war, and swept the central Mediterranean. The initiative was never to be surrendered.

3. The Fight Begins

MUSSOLINI probably declared war in anticipation of a cheap and early German-Italian victory over France, and on the assumption that the collapse of the British Empire would follow without much exertion on the part of Italy. Only this can explain the absence of any spectacular offensive at sea, accompanying or following the declaration of war.

The British Fleet instantly grasped the initiative. At dawn on 11th June the Commander-in-Chief put to sea with the battleships Warspite and Malaya, the cruisers Orion, Neptune, Sydney, Liverpool and Gloucester, the carrier Eagle and a force of screening destroyers. This force swept the central Mediterranean as far as the south coast of Italy, and returned to fuel without sighting a hostile vessel, although the destroyer Voyager accounted for an Italian submarine. A French cruiser squadron searched the Aegean with similar result.

In the course of this operation the Liverpool and the Gloucester were detached to attack any sea forces at Tobruk. They shelled a flotilla of minesweepers off the harbour in the face of a heavy fire from shore batteries. They were unaware that a British patrol of Hussars, a hundred miles inside the enemy lines, happened to be on the beach in the vicinity and was watching the incident.

There followed a succession of sorties and sweeps by cruisers, and unremitting submarine hunts which disposed of a number of Italian U-boats, but no contact was made with enemy surface forces. In the meanwhile, Italian shipping in the eastern Mediterranean and Red Sea was rounded up by patrol vessels. Other shipping started moving again, unescorted.

The Italian attack on France at the moment she was reeling before Germany's terrible mechanised onslaught produced the collapse that might be expected of a man simultaneously stabbed between the shoulders and struck in the eyes with a knuckle-duster. On Sunday, 23rd June, it became known that France was about to sign an armistice with Germany. The units of the French Fleet in the Mediterranean were recalled to their harbours, full of fight, but bewildered and dismayed by the incredible disaster to their nation. On 25th June the French Government gave the order to cease fire. The shores friendly to the British Fleet had shrunk to the coasts of Egypt and Palestine, and the islands of Cyprus and Malta. There were no wardens of the western basin, and henceforward the British units faced the enemy alone.

Malta was being bombed incessantly and sporadic raids were made on Alexandria; but it was essential that shipping should be resumed, both to link the Aegean and Red Sea convoys, and to maintain communications between Malta, Alexandria and the Suez Canal. In an operation covering a Malta convoy at the end of June our cruisers sighted three enemy destroyers off Cape Matapan. They sank one at long range as they fled

westward in the failing light. The destroyer Dainty and her flotilla ran into a number of Italian submarines off Crete and disposed of three in quick succession. A flying boat accounted for a fourth and a probable fifth. It was like stamping on a viper's nest.

About the same time, a powerful force of capital ships, with the aircraft-carrier Ark Royal and screening destroyers, assembled at Gibraltar under the command of Admiral Sir James Somerville. It was known as Force

H, and was available for the defence of the western basin of the Mediterranean, or for operations in the Atlantic. It was destined to play a considerable part in the interception and destruction of the German battleship Bismarck.

In the background of these events France lay abased by her betrayers. Misery and unrest swept the wardrooms and mess-decks of the French Fleet, sapping its robust fighting spirit. It gradually became evident that the French sailors had only one unifying impulse,

to return to their home ports. The seizure of these ships by Germany would then be inevitable.

It was hoped that a satisfactory solution of the problem, consonant with French honour, would be reached by negotiation. This failed at Oran, where the bulk of the French Fleet was lying, and Force H was sent there in token of the desperately serious intention of the British Government to prevent the ships from falling into German hands. Force H

THE SCALES TILT. When France fell, all coasts but those of Egypt, Palestine, Gibraltar and the islands of Malta and Cyprus were closed to the British Fleet, though later Greece became our ally. This map shows the position in March, 1941, by which time the coastline of Cyrenaica, following General Wavell's advance, was also under our control. Allied coastline is shown light, neutral striped and enemy dark.

DESTROYED AND DESTROYER

These remarkable pictures show the death of an Italian submarine, the Gondar. It is the 30th September, 1940. She has been hunted for hours through the central Mediterranean by the destroyer Stuart, until at last depth charges force her to blow her tanks and break surface, *left*. *Below*, members of her crew can be seen swimming to life-lines lowered from the Stuart. The Stuart's davits are swung out, and one of her boats is away rescuing other survivors.

was eventually compelled to open fire, sinking a battleship and damaging by air attack a battle-cruiser of the Strasbourg class.

At Alexandria, after prolonged discussion between the French Admiral Godfroi and the British Commanders-in-Chief, the French men-of-war in that port were demilitarised by their own officers and men, most of whom were subsequently repatriated. Thus the curtain fell on one of the sorriest dramas ever enacted in war.

4. First Clash of the Battle Fleets

Two important convoys from Malta, one with evacuated women and children, and the other with stores, had been planned early in July. On the 7th the Commander-in-Chief took the Fleet to sea with the object of protecting the convoys from attack by Italian forces. These sailed in three groups:

Force A. Vice-Admiral J. C. Tovey (commanding Light Forces and Second in Command) flying his flag in the Orion, with the cruisers Neptune, Sydney, Gloucester and Liverpool, and the Australian flotilla-leader Stuart.

Force B. The Commander-in-Chief in the Warspite, screened by five destroyers.

Force C. The battleships Royal Sovereign and Malaya, the carrier Eagle and a screening flotilla, under Rear-Admiral H. D. Pridham-Wippell.

They set a north-westerly course at 20 knots. Just before midnight, the Hasty, one of Force C's destroyer screen, swung out of line and beat the life out of an Italian submarine with depth charges; an hour later, hurrying along to rejoin her flotilla, she attacked and damaged a second.

All the next day Italian bombers from the Dodecanese swept over the Fleet in waves. Between noon and 6 p.m. seven attacks were made on the flagship. About fifty heavy bombs were dropped. None hit. Force C had eighty bombs rained down on it with similar negative results. In spite of the intensity of this high-level bombing, the only hit regis-

THUNDER OF BATTLE. On 8th and 9th July, 1940, came the first trial of strength and seamanship between the British and Italian Battle Fleets. The action began with a heavy enemy air attack ; bombs are here seen falling clear of the stern of the battleship Royal Sovereign. On the right is the aircraft-carrier Eagle.

tered by the enemy was on the cruiser Gloucester, whose Captain was amongst eighteen officers and men killed; nine were wounded.

In the afternoon of 8th July, a patrolling flying boat reported an enemy force of three battleships, six cruisers and seven destroyers about a hundred miles to the north-west of Benghazi, on a northerly course. It was probable that they were returning from a similar mission to that of the British Fleet, the covering of an important convoy. The Commander-in-Chief held on his course,

which would interpose his fleet between the enemy and his base in Italy.

The Eagle's aircraft went up at dawn on the following day to reconnoitre, but it was an R.A.F. flying boat from Malta that first sighted the enemy fleet. Subsequent reports located a further large force of cruisers and destroyers in the vicinity. About noon the Italians were about ninety miles to the westward of our forces, and the Commander-in-Chief decided to launch an air striking-force from the Eagle; but the shadowing air-craft had the bad luck to lose touch with the enemy, who just then appeared to have turned to the southward. The striking-force failed to locate its quarry. A shadower regained touch with the enemy battleships in the afternoon and again the air striking-force went off. It returned safely having scored a hit on a cruiser. The enemy fleet appeared to consist of two battleships, the Cavour and the Cesare, twelve cruisers and twenty destroyers; they were hugging the coast of Calabria.

Shortly after 3 p.m., six 8-in. gun cruisers and a number of destroyers were sighted steering east of north. A few minutes later the Italian battle fleet was sighted to the westward by the Neptune. Captain R. C. O'Conor thus had the privilege of signalling " Enemy battle fleet in sight " for the first time in the Mediterranean since the Napoleonic wars.

The British 6-in. gun cruisers were outranged and came under heavy fire. The comparatively slow Royal Sovereign limited the speed of the Battle Fleet, but the Commander-in-Chief in the Warspite, ignoring the odds against him, instantly went to the support of his desperately outnumbered and outranged cruisers. A few long-range salvoes from the Warspite seemed to discourage the enemy, who turned away. Throughout the action Captain A. R. M. Bridge of the Eagle continued to launch a succession of flights of torpedo-carrying Swordfish in incessant sorties against the enemy. This was the first time an aircraft-carrier had worked with a fleet in battle: it was a day full of precedents, one way and another.

After a short lull, the Warspite and the Malaya engaged the two Italian battleships, and the Warspite scored a hit on the Cesare at the enormous range of 26,000 yards. This had the disconcerting effect of making the enemy battleships turn away under cover of smoke, the enemy cruisers following suit.

The Royal Sovereign, owing to her slow speed, did not get into this swiftly moving action. To cover their fleet's retreat the Italian destroyers made a half-hearted movement towards the British force, emitting volumes of black smoke. The British cruisers and destroyers rushed to meet them, but before they could get within range the enemy, having launched a torpedo attack, retreated into the dense smoke-screen that had already swallowed the Italian battleships and cruisers. British and light forces chased them to the edge of it, while the Commander-in-Chief in the Warspite prowled round the windward side like a terrier at a burning haystack. When eventually the smoke cleared, all enemy forces were out of sight ; bombing attacks from the Italian coast then began.

Between 4.40 and 7.12 p.m. at least nine attacks took place, probably a hundred aircraft participating. Undeterred by this bombardment the Fleet held on towards the coast for an hour in the vain hope that the enemy would take advantage of his numerical superiority and renew the fight. When Calabria was in sight, however, it became clear that he could not be intercepted before reaching Messina. Course was altered to the south-eastward to open the land, and at 9.15 p.m. the Commander-in-Chief set a course for Malta. With the exception of the Gloucester, the Fleet had suffered neither damage nor casualties, and after fuelling at Malta it resumed protection of the east-bound convoys. The latter, although bombed all the way, reached Alexandria unscathed.

This action of 9th July has been described in some detail because it was the first contact with the Italian fleet and reveals the morale and strategy of the opposing forces in the Mediterranean.

The British Fleet's control of the narrow seas had been challenged by superior surface forces, and these had retreated to their harbours in the face of accurate long-range fire.

At a range of thirteen miles it must have seemed uncannily accurate. On two occasions in the ensuing months (31st August and 30th September) the Italian battle fleet was again in the vicinity of the British Fleet; and although on each occasion the latter was cumbered with a convoy and in the second encounter our battleships were outnumbered by five to two, the Italian fleet avoided action as if tacitly accepting British mastery of the eastern Mediterranean.

The action is also significant as an indication of the weapon in which Italy had decided to put her trust. The Warspite and her attendant destroyers were attacked by bombers twenty-two times, Force C fifteen times; altogether nearly 400 bombs were dropped on the British Fleet during its return to Alexandria, without causing damage or casualties. The new weapon had had every chance to prove itself a substitute for sea power and had apparently failed ; in the confusion of the enemy's retreat to the Straits of Messina the Italian bombers were twice observed to be attacking their own fleet. The German dive-bombers had not yet appeared on the scene.

Italy's lines of communication with the Dodecanese through the southern Aegean continued to be a hunting ground for our light forces. On 18th July four destroyers under Commander H. St. L. Nicolson went off to search for enemy submarines north of Crete, while the Australian cruiser Sydney, commanded by Captain J. A. Collins, Royal Australian Navy, with the destroyer Havock in company, followed him on a raid against Italian shipping in the Gulf of Athens. This was the intention of the outing, but in the misty dawn of the following day two Italian cruisers were sighted to the westward by our destroyers at a range of ten miles. The Sydney was about forty-five miles away, somewhere to the northward. Commander Nicolson, outranged and heavily outgunned, turned his force in that direction, hoping to draw the Italian cruisers after him

AN ITALIAN BATTLESHIP IS HIT. The Warspite scores a direct hit on the Cesare at the extreme range of nearly 15 miles. The picture shows a gun-turret destroyed and the smoke-stack blown open. After this hit, the Italians turned for home.

within range of the Sydney's guns. He succeeded, and at 8.30 a.m. the Sydney sighted the enemy in pursuit of the flotilla— H.M.S. Hyperion, Hero, Hasty and Ilex— who were under a heavy but fortunately inaccurate long-range fire. During the course of this pursuit, the Hasty, who was the last in the line, made a signal to the Hero, her next ahead. " Don't look round now," blinked her signal lamp, while Italian shells pitched round them in all directions, " but I think we are being followed." Three

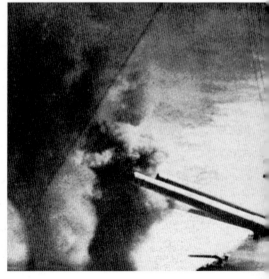

minutes later the Sydney began shooting and the destroyers, having achieved their object, turned to attack the enemy with torpedoes.

The Italian cruisers turned away immediately and the action became a pursuit. The rear cruiser, the Bartolomeo Colleoni, was repeatedly hit and finally lay stopped, flames and smoke pouring from her. Ordering the destroyers to finish her off, the Sydney continued in chase of her fleeing consort. The interior of the Bartolomeo Colleoni was a raging furnace when the Hyperion and the Ilex closed to sink her with torpedoes, but her ensign still flew at the peak. She sank with it flying. While the Havock picked up survivors (she was attacked by enemy bombers in the process) the remaining destroyers went off after the Sydney to join in the pursuit. Although repeatedly hit, the second enemy cruiser continued to draw ahead and was eventually lost in the Mediterranean summer haze. The Sydney was running out of ammunition and decided to abandon the chase.

The British force was heavily bombed on the way back to Alexandria, which, as somebody put it, was just too bad for the prisoners, who had had a long and tiring day. The Havock was holed with splinters from a near miss which slightly reduced her speed, but she reached port without further mishap. There were no other casualties.

On receiving news of the engagement just described, the Fleet put to sea and swept towards the north-west. The fugitive Italian cruiser when last seen was steering south, and it was thought might be taking refuge in Tobruk. The Eagle, therefore, supported by the 1st Battle Squadron and a screen of destroyers, went to the westward and in the early hours of 20th July flew off six torpedo-carrying Swordfish to attack shipping in the harbour. The cruiser was not there, but a 5,000 ton tanker was, and a torpedo sent her up in a sheet of flame ; two smaller vessels were also destroyed.

A squadron of the Eagle's Swordfish had

IN FULL RETREAT. Under cover of a smoke-screen, but firing her heavy guns, an Italian battleship, *below left*, begins the retreat from the smaller British force. *Below right*, the action is nearly over. An Italian Cavour-class battleship is firing directly astern at her pursuers. The range is now extreme, but the shells from the pursuing British ships are falling close.

END OF AN ITALIAN CRUISER. The Bartolomeo Colleoni, sighted and chased by H.M.A.S. Sydney on 19th July, 1940, is seen behind a picket-fence of shell-bursts from the Australian cruiser.

HER BOWS BLOWN OFF, and with smoke and flames pouring from her, the Bartolomeo Colleoni, *above*, lies stopped. *Below*, the last great explosion, as she is finished off with torpedoes.

earlier in the month torpedoed two destroyers and two merchant ships in the harbour, and this second attack resulted in Tobruk being abandoned by Italy as a base for her light forces, and as a supply base for her army.

The Fleet returned to harbour in time to clear lower deck and cheer the Sydney and her destroyers when the little force came into harbour with 545 prisoners. The King sent his personal congratulations and awarded the C.B. to Captain Collins; Commander Nicolson was granted a bar to his D.S.O.

5. Mussolini Moves on Land

AT THE END of July enemy air reconnaissance over Alexandria became more frequent. The Italians seized the opportunity when the Fleet was known to be in harbour to slip fast convoys of reinforcements into Libya. Alexandria is three times as far from Tripoli as Sicily. The defences of Malta were still too weak for the island to be used as a base from which our light forces could operate against these convoys. The few submarines then available had to do what they could in those dangerously transparent waters to stem the flow of troops and stores into North Africa. So slender were our resources in aircraft capable of aggression against enemy sea forces, that about this time, when the Italians were building up an army to invade Egypt, the control of the central Mediterranean was very largely in their hands. With the forces at his command there was very little that the Commander-in-Chief, watching the Adriatic, the

Aegean and the eastern Mediterranean, could do about it.

By the middle of August the Italian army was massed in sufficiently large concentrations along the coast to make it worth attacking them from the sea. The Battle Fleet sallied forth to Bardia and for twenty minutes poured an appalling deluge of 15-in. and 6-in. high-explosive shell into forts, encampments, barracks and batteries. The place had already received two similar visitations from cruiser and destroyer forces and one from the French battleship Lorraine. A week later a surprise night-attack by destroyers beat up the seaplane base at Bomba; three Swordfish of the Fleet Air Arm sank two submarines, a destroyer and a depot ship anchored in the bay. The Ladybird, a diminutive gunboat which had spent most of her life on the Yangtse, took advantage of her shallow draught to enter Bardia harbour itself. She spent twenty-five minutes shelling the place at almost point-blank range, her Captain, Lieutenant-Commander Blackburn, coolly selecting the targets for her 6-in. gun by searchlight, and silencing any shore guns that were able to range on her.

The Ladybird was subsequently joined by one of her Yangtse sisters, the Aphis, and the pair of them went tripping along the flank of the advancing Italian army, ignoring bombs and torpedoes from the air, harassing their lines of communication and rudely interfering with their sleep. On one occasion, the Ladybird reported passing through a controlled minefield. A number of mines went up around her. " No avoiding action was necessary," she observed primly in her report on the operation. The Ladybird and the Aphis will be met again later, on the flank of the retreating enemy.

To remedy the situation in the central Mediterranean and in the air generally, it was decided to reinforce the Fleet with the battleship Valiant, the new aircraft-carrier Illustrious and the anti-aircraft cruisers Calcutta and Coventry. They passed through the Mediterranean from west to east during 30th August–5th September, supported as far as Sardinia by Admiral Somerville's powerful Force H, and met south of Sicily by the Commander-in-Chief's fleet from Alexandria. This was the first occasion on which our forces on a large scale passed through the narrows between Sicily and Cape Bon.

Opportunity was taken to convoy quantities of stores and reinforcements from Britain to Malta, and to pass a convoy there from Alexandria, covered by the Mediterranean Fleet. It was a delicately timed operation, commencing simultaneously from either end of a 1,700 mile line, and it was entirely suc-

cessful, although on the second day at sea the enemy's battle fleet was sighted in the vicinity by reconnaissance aircraft from the Eagle. No attack on the convoy materialised, however, and the enemy retreated.

S.S. Cornwall, one of the ships in the Malta convoy, was bombed on the passage. Both her guns were destroyed, her steering gear was totally disabled, she was set on fire aft, holed below the waterline, and her wireless put out of action. After about a quarter of an hour's pardonable delay, during which the magazine blew up and the fire spread to the hold, her master, Captain F. C. Pretty, signalled that he found he could steer with his main engines, and got his ship back on to her

THE BATTLE FLEET TAKES A HAND. The battleships Malaya and Ramillies, with a County class cruiser, steam to sea in mid-August, 1940, to pour a deluge of shells on Bardia and Fort Capuzzo, where the Italian army is gathering for its first advance into Egypt.

course. In an hour, during which ready-use ammunition continued to explode at intervals, the fire was got under control.

It was eventually extinguished, the leak was stopped, and Captain Pretty continued to steer with his screws and no rudder, maintaining his position and speed in the convoy through a heavy sea until arrival at Malta two days later. This feat of seamanship avoided delaying the convoy and upsetting the time-table of the whole complex operation, with incalculable consequences.

By way of immediately asserting her presence in the Mediterranean, the Illustrious turned aside before reaching Alexandria to enable her Swordfish bombers to attack a

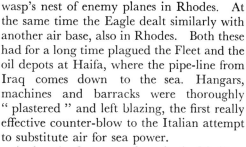

wasp's nest of enemy planes in Rhodes. At the same time the Eagle dealt similarly with another air base, also in Rhodes. Both these had for a long time plagued the Fleet and the oil depots at Haifa, where the pipe-line from Iraq comes down to the sea. Hangars, machines and barracks were thoroughly " plastered " and left blazing, the first really effective counter-blow to the Italian attempt to substitute air for sea power.

And so the first year of war in the Mediterranean passed into history. We had lost the cruiser Calypso, sunk by a torpedo, and the destroyer Hostile, which was mined. Five of our submarines had failed to return from their patrols, but we balanced the account by destroying sixteen of the enemy's that were operating in the Mediterranean and the Red Sea. The exploits of our submarines in the eastern Mediterranean would fill a separate volume, and for this reason have not been given their due throughout the course of the present narrative.

On 13th September the loudly heralded Italian invasion of Egypt commenced. It got as far as Sidi Barrani, where the enemy paused. On 17th September two squadrons of Swordfish flew off from the Illustrious and attacked Benghazi, which the Italians had used as a supply base since the Eagle's Swordfish had made Tobruk too hot for their shipping. Taking advantage of a full moon these squadrons mined the entrance and sank a destroyer and two merchant ships. Further casualties are believed to have followed later. Thanks to its reinforced air-arm the Fleet's striking power was reaching out farther and farther afield.

From the sea, destroyers and the imperturbable Ladybird carried out surprise night bombardments with such persistence that the Australian Captain commanding the destroyer flotilla, who was in charge of these junketings, at last reported regretfully, " All targets driven inland, leaving practically nothing to be engaged from seaward." The loader of one destroyer's foremost 4·7-in. gun, having wearily slammed something in the region of the sixtieth round into the breech, was heard to mutter an apt but unprintable comment as the gun fired the last shot at the scuttling Italians.

The Commander-in-Chief had hitherto been handicapped by having to combine attempts to bring the Italian battle fleet to action with the necessity for covering valuable and essential convoys to Malta. If the Italians had been eager for battle, he would have found himself in the situation of a man trying to fight someone heavier than himself, with a woman on his arm. On 30th September, covering an important convoy to Malta with two battleships, he found himself in the vicinity of the Italian fleet with five battleships. They avoided action, however. These were odds he was continually forced to accept, because if the Italian main fleet could be destroyed, the west to east sea route through the Mediterranean would be reopened.

The addition of the Illustrious to the Fleet, however, materially altered the situation. Her Fulmar fighters made the shadowing of the Fleet by enemy reconnaissance machines

a most hazardous and costly adventure; the continuous menace from bombing squadrons based on Italy, Sicily, Libya and the Dodecanese against the Fleet and convoys, was now to some extent countered by the presence with the Fleet of an armoured mobile aerodrome. If the enemy fleet declined action on the high seas the alternative was to seek it out and destroy it in harbour. The answer to a gun-shy enemy was the Fleet Air Arm.

Taranto, the main base of the Italian fleet, was kept under constant observation, and early in October there were three Cavour or Duilio and two Littorio-class battleships there, with two 8-in. gun and six 6-in. gun cruisers, and about twenty destroyers, in the harbour. An operation against Taranto was planned for 21st October, the anniversary of the Battle of Trafalgar, but for various reasons had to be postponed.

As an immediate alternative, the Commander-in-Chief took the Fleet to sea to tempt the enemy's superior forces to battle, and as usual to cover important convoys. No contact was made with the enemy's main fleet but, while returning from Malta, cover-

CLOSE BOMBARDMENT: a C class cruiser comes right in to bombard Bardia, the Italian strong-point on the high Libyan coast.

ing an east-bound convoy, Captain E. D. B. McCarthy, commanding the cruiser Ajax, sighted two enemy destroyers by moonlight on the night of 11th October and engaged them at short range. One was put out of action and left blazing fiercely, while the Ajax turned her attention to the other. She blew up under heavy fire. A third destroyer was then sighted and, after a short engagement, also blew up. The Ajax then went in pursuit of two more enemy ships, which escaped under cover of smoke. The formation of a smoke-screen by the Italians, directly fire was opened on them, had become almost a reflex action, like a squid ejecting ink on sighting an enemy.

The burning destroyer (identified as the Artagliere) was sighted and reported by a Sunderland flying boat on reconnaissance from Malta early next morning. She was in tow of another destroyer which shortly afterwards, on being attacked by aircraft, slipped her and fled to the northward. The cruiser York was detached to the position of the crippled destroyer, whose crew waved sheets and towels in token of surrender. The fire had been extinguished, and her ship's company was with difficulty persuaded to abandon her. Bearing in mind the fate of the Havock—she was bombed by enemy formations while rescuing survivors from the Colleoni on 19th July—Captain R. Portal of the York decided not to stop and transfer the prisoners. Rafts were therefore dropped astern of the destroyer ; and when her crew had at last reluctantly taken to the water she was sunk by gunfire.

While the Ajax's spirited action was in progress, Rear-Admiral A. L. St. G. Lyster, Commanding Aircraft Carriers, was detached to revisit the Dodecanese with the carriers Illustrious and Eagle. On 13th October they carried out an attack on Leros, taking the airfield and garrison completely by surprise. Ninety-two bombs were dropped on hangars, workshops and fuel tanks by naval Swordfish with results that must have been profoundly discouraging to the enemy.

At three o'clock on the morning of 28th October, Italy delivered an ultimatum to Greece demanding occupation of Crete, Corfu, Salonika, Patras and other strategic points. The President of the Council refused these outrageous demands and told the Italian Minister that they amounted to a declaration of war. He appealed to Britain for immediate naval help to defend Corfu.

The first necessity was the establishment of an advanced fuelling base at Suda Bay in Crete, and a convoy of tankers was sent there the next day, covered by a force of cruisers and destroyers, while the Commander-in-Chief cruised to the westward with the Battle Fleet. The disembarkation of troops and stores at Suda Bay had been completed and some form of defence established by 1st November despite bombing attacks; in the meanwhile, the Italian invaders of Greece were meeting with an unexpected and ferocious resistance.

With Italy's utterly unprovoked onslaught against Greece, the background of the naval war changed once more. We had again an ally in the Mediterranean, but owing to the smallness of her navy, the defence of the islands and coasts of Greece against Italy laid fresh responsibilities on the British Fleet. Convoys carrying troops and stores to Greece's aid had to be run through the Aegean and escorted past the hornets' nests of the Dodecanese. Defences had to be provided for Crete, and all the time Malta, the beleaguered fortress to the west, had to be sustained. It was no time for waiting to see what was going to happen next. In Greece and Libya Italian armies were advancing ; more than quarter of a million enemy troops faced our weak garrisons in the Sudan and Kenya. Italy had to be punched in the *solar plexus* there and then, and as the Naval Commander-in-Chief saw it the Italian *solar plexus* was the Italian battle fleet. The Fleet Air Arm's moment had come to deliver that blow. The war was about to enter a new phase.

THE ARTAGLIERE'S TOMBSTONE OF SMOKE.
On the moonlit night of 11th October, 1940, the cruiser Ajax sighted three enemy destroyers, sank two, and put the third, the Artagliere, out of action. The next day the cruiser York found her, and sank her by gunfire after rafts had been dropped for her crew. *Below*, she is badly on fire astern. *Right*, she blows up and disappears.

6. Cunningham Strikes:
the Swoop on Taranto

ALTHOUGH Italian seamen have never lacked courage, her Navy has not the professional and psychological outlook of the bluewater sailor; and under Mussolini's regime political uncertainty must inevitably have penetrated the wardrooms and mess-decks of the fleet. When that happened, it was perhaps no longer completely reliable as a weapon in war.

A suspicion of this may have decided Italy to put her faith in air power and to take no undue risks with her fleet. Indeed, for a nation which had air bases actual or potential straddling the central Mediterranean and stretching along the entire Libyan coast, this must have seemed the obvious strategy. The only answer we had was the aircraft-carrier and the Fleet Air Arm.

Although Force H at Gibraltar had one foot in the western Mediterranean, its primary function was to seek out and destroy enemy raiders in the Atlantic. For this purpose a carrier was necessary, and the Ark Royal formed part of this striking-force.

The fleet in the eastern Mediterranean had, however, no carrier until the Eagle joined in May 1940 from the East Indies, in command of Captain A. R. M. Bridge. Her relatively small fuel endurance was adequate for the narrow seas; but she was twenty years old, her speed and armour were below modern requirements and she had none of the up-to-date appliances of the latest carriers. She brought with her two squadrons of Swordfish, and she later acquired four Gladiators as the basis of a fighter squadron. There were no fighter pilots on board, but the Commander (Flying) of the Eagle, Commander C. L. Keighley-Peach, was an "old lag" of Fleet Air Arm fighters. ("Old lag" is their phrase; actually he was thirty-eight.) For a while he went up alone to defend the Fleet. Later he trained two of the bomber pilots as fighter pilots; the three of them, until they were reinforced by more machines and pilots, were all the Fleet had in the way of air defence against bombers and shadowers. Between them they accounted for eleven enemy aircraft and somehow contrived to preserve the Fleet from major casualty. On one occasion the "old lag" went up alone with a bullet still in his thigh from a previous encounter and shot down an enemy machine.

During these months the Eagle's Swordfish, operating from unaccustomed desert landing grounds, were a scourge to the enemy's Libyan ports.

The Illustrious, it will be remembered, arrived in the Mediterranean on 1st September. Not only was she the last word in carriers, but she had on board in addition to her torpedo-bomber Swordfish, a squadron of Fulmars, the new fleet fighters. The former she blooded in the Dodecanese on her passage to Alexandria in company with the Eagle. By the end of October the Illustrious's fighters were able, for the first time, to prevent enemy bombers from penetrating the fringes of the Fleet.

The Rear-Admiral Commanding Aircraft Carriers and Captain D. W. Boyd, in command of the Illustrious, arrived on the station with their own ideas for an attack with torpedoes on the enemy's battle fleet in Taranto harbour. As has been noted, it coincided with the strategical necessity of the moment, which was to smite Italy afloat. Other commitments postponed the operation, but 11th November was finally chosen as the date.

One of the preliminaries of an attack of this kind is a detailed photographic reconnaissance of the objectives: it was necessary to know almost up to the last moment what ships were in harbour, and also their positions and berthing. This reconnaissance was carried out by Royal Air Force aircraft from Malta, who continued to take photographs, in spite of considerable fighter opposition, up to 10th November. A subsequent reconnaissance by the R.A.F. on the 11th confirmed that no important movements had taken place. To make doubly sure of the quarry, the Gulf of Taranto was patrolled by the R.A.F. until the attack actually commenced, to ensure that nothing left the harbour unobserved.

The operation fitted in with convoy movements to Greece, Crete and Malta, requiring the presence of the Fleet at sea. The Commander-in-Chief sailed on 6th November, but the Eagle had to be left behind. The near misses she had sustained in bombing attacks had made some of her petrol tanks defective. Eight of her crews and some Swordfish were, however, transferred to the Illustrious before she sailed.

On 8th November a formation of seven S.79s approached the Fleet and was promptly attacked by three of the Illustrious's Fulmars. They shot down two and the remainder jettisoned their bombs and fled. A venturesome Cant.506B shadower was shot down the next day. On the morning of 11th one of the Illustrious's planes fetched the latest photographs of Taranto from Malta.

They showed five battleships in the outer harbour—three of the Cavour or Duilio class and two of the Littorio—and three cruisers protected by nets. There were also some cruisers and destroyers in the Mar Piccolo. The crews of the Swordfish fell on the photographs with stereoscopic glasses, thanking heaven and the R.A.F.

In the morning a Swordfish on reconnaissance had a mishap and made a forced landing in the sea, fortunately in the vicinity of the cruiser Gloucester. The crew were rescued, but they were to have taken part in the attack that night, and their dismay at the

THE SHIELD AROUND TARANTO. This Italian propaganda picture, put out in 1940, was designed to show Italy's invulnerability. The Sicilian Channel and the Straits of Otranto are completely blocked. Above all, the naval base of Taranto, inside the "heel," is shielded behind impenetrable defences. There Italy's fleet would surely be safe.

prospect of missing the entertainment so touched the heart of the Gloucester's Captain that he gave orders for them to be flown back to their ship in his Walrus.

In the afternoon the watchful R.A.F. patrol in the Gulf of Taranto reported

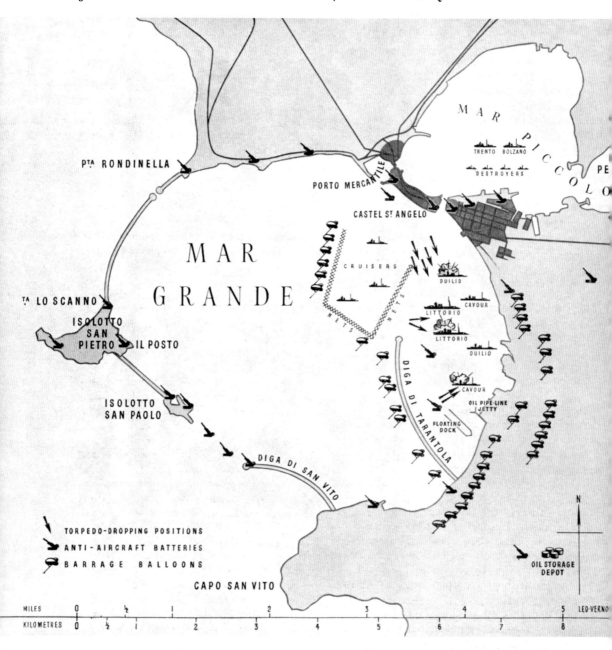

THE ENEMY'S HIDE-OUT. Taranto, where the Fleet Air Arm sought out the Italian fleet in their own anchorage. The map shows the inner harbour, the Mar Piccolo, where Italian cruisers were successfully bombed, the outer harbour, the Mar Grande, where half of Italy's battle fleet was put out of action by torpedoes, and the oil-storage depot which was bombed by the flare-dropping planes after they had lighted up the target for the rest.

another battleship entering harbour. That brought the total up to six and the bomber pilots and observers on board the Illustrious rejoiced grimly. Italy's eggs were at last all in one basket.

At 6 p.m. on 11th November the great moment in the history of the Fleet Air Arm arrived. The Rear-Admiral Aircraft Carriers, in the Illustrious, supported by the 3rd Cruiser Squadron and four destroyers, was detached to proceed in execution of previous orders.

To this end the Fleet Air Arm had patiently planned, experimented and designed through years of a peace they knew was not peace at all. Many of their young men had given their lives in the process, believing it was worth it, and the time had come to justify their beliefs:

He either fears his fate too much
Or his deserts are small
Who dare not put it to the touch
To win or lose it all.

" Good luck, then," signalled the Commander-in-Chief to Rear-Admiral Lyster, as they parted company from the Fleet, " to your lads in their enterprise. Their success may well have a most important bearing on the course of the war in the Mediterranean."

Apart from the passage of convoys between Alexandria and Greece and Malta, important reinforcements for the Fleet, consisting of the battleship Barham and the cruisers Berwick and Glasgow, were due to pass from west to east in the course of this operation. The defences of Malta had by now become sufficiently formidable to enable Admiral Ford to dispense with the monitor Terror, and this opportunity was taken to transfer her to the new fuelling base at Suda Bay to hold it against air attack till the shore defences were completed.

In addition to all these immensely complex operations, covering most of the Mediterranean with a wide succession of subsidiary movements, the Second-in-Command, Vice-Admiral Pridham-Wippell, was dispatched with the 7th Cruiser Squadron and two destroyers to raid the Straits of Otranto. He parted from the main Fleet for this purpose during the afternoon of 11th.

While these preliminaries were in progress a force of Italian aircraft was co-operating with the Germans in a daylight attack on London. The Italians lost seven bombers and six fighters, which would perhaps have been better employed defending their fleet from what was coming to it.

By 8 p.m. the Illustrious and her escort had reached the position, 170 miles from Taranto, from which it was intended to launch the attack. There were to be two main assaults. The plan was the same for both: preceded by aircraft dropping flares and bombs along the eastern side of the Mar Grande, and by dive-bombing attacks on the cruisers and destroyers in the Mar Piccolo, the striking-force of torpedo carriers was to attack the battleships from the west and north-west.

The first squadron began to leave the Illustrious's flight deck at 8.35 p.m. Veils of thin cloud drifted across the moon at intervals. In five minutes the whole striking-force was in the air. The aircraft formed up on their leader, Lieutenant-Commander K. Williamson, and set a course for Taranto.

Shortly before 11 p.m. the defences of the harbour heard them and opened fire. The flare-dropper was detached to pass over Capo San Vito, and he came in at 7,500 feet, dropping his flares at half-mile intervals. Having provided what appeared to be a satisfactory illumination for the proceedings, he cruised round for a quarter of an hour in search of a target, and finally made a dive-bombing attack through the barrage on to an oil-storage depot. He was followed down by the other flare-dropper who added his bombs to the first, and the pair of them returned to the carrier.

The four aircraft detailed to attack shipping in the Mar Piccolo set the seaplane base on fire and bombed cruisers and destroyers

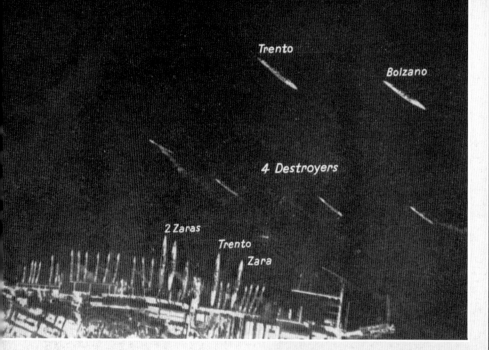

Trento

Bolzano

4 Destroyers

2 Zaras

Trento

Zara

THE CRUISER CASUALTIES. The smaller photograph shows the inner harbour at Taranto the day before the Fleet Air Arm attack. It was taken on 10th November by an R.A.F. reconnaissance aircraft. Italian heavy cruisers and destroyers are lying snugly at anchor. The large photograph was taken the day after the attack. The two cruisers, of the Bolzano and Trento classes, heeled over and heavily damaged, are lying in pools of their own oil. One has a tug giving assistance. The other Trento-class cruiser has been moved out from the dockside. The Zara-class cruisers are undamaged —they had their turn at Matapan,

Oil Pipe line
jetty

Destroyers

Cavour

Duilio

Littorio

Littorio

Cavour

Duilio

ALL HER EGGS IN ONE BASKET. In the above picture, all six of Italy's battleships are shown safely at anchor in the outer harbour at Taranto. The photograph was taken by R.A.F. reconnaissance aircraft on 10th November. Next day the Fleet Air Arm attacked and disabled half of them with torpedoes. The two photographs on the right-hand page, taken on 12th November, show the damage done. In the larger of the two pictures, the bows of the Cavour-class battleship (nearest to the pipe-line jetty in the reconnaissance photograph) are now aground; she has heeled over board with her stern and the starboard side of her upp under water. Great smudges of fuel oil come from h *Right,* one of the Littorio-class battleships (the lowe the reconnaissance photograph) with her bows partly She is surrounded by auxiliary craft trying to salva on her port side a tanker engaged in pumping ope on her starboard side a couple of tugs, an ocea submarine (presumably supplying the crippled sh

Tugs
← Submarine
← Naval Auxiliary
Tanker

ic power from her batteries, her own dynamos having
[ ] put out of action) and a naval auxiliary. The diagonal
[ ]ings on the decks of these battleships are aircraft recog-
[ ] stripes, borne by all Italian naval units so that their
[ ] airmen shall recognise them. The third Italian
[ ]ship that was known to have been hit—one of the
[ ] class—was also observed the next day with her bows
[ ]nd and with salvage vessels alongside. After Taranto,
[ ] removed the remainder of her battle fleet to Naples.

alongside. They too returned "without incident," as their phrase goes; the ferocious barrage of high explosive, pom-pom and machine-gun fire through which they made their get-away does not come within the classification of an incident.

Lieutenant-Commander Williamson did not return to the Illustrious. The Squadron-Commander was last seen by one of the torpedo carriers over the island of San Pietro. At this point the second Swordfish dived to the attack. The pilot skimmed the breakwater between the balloon cables, torpedoed the battleship to the northward of the floating dock and returned the way he had come through A.A. fire that was, he admits, intense.

His companion in the sub-flight followed with another torpedo at the same Cavour-class battleship. The other sub-flight concentrated on the Littorios, one of which was hit. With the exception of their leader, the whole striking-force returned safely to the carrier.

In the meanwhile the second striking-force was being flown off. The last up from the hangar, taxying into position in the darkness, damaged the fabric of one wing. It happened to be manned by the pair who had that morning made a forced landing in the sea and been rescued by the Gloucester. To be baulked of the adventure a second time was beyond the limit of endurance. While one rushed the aircraft back into the hangar for repair, the other entreated the Captain to allow them to follow the striking-force by themselves. In sheer pity he let them go and a quarter of an hour later they took off.

Twenty minutes after the departure of the second striking-force one of the Swordfish, owing to a mishap, was forced to return to the carrier, and to the disgust of the crew took no part in the attack. The others reached their objective, illuminated by flares, fires and anti-aircraft fire, at 11.50 p.m. The tactics of the first attack were repeated. Two flare-droppers illuminated the harbour from the east and south-east, and then dive-bombed the oil depot. They returned safely, although one reported bursts of A.A. shell "particularly close," which is probably no exaggeration. The belated aircraft arrived while the attack by torpedo carriers was in full swing—so apparently was the A.A. fire. The pilot came in over the land to the eastward and selected the cruisers and destroyers in the Mar Piccolo as his target. A stick of bombs was dropped on the cruisers and this aircraft also returned safely. The pilot noted as he turned that one of the battleships was blazing furiously.

The torpedo carriers were led to the attack by the Squadron-Commander, Lieutenant-Commander J. W. Hale. These all selected the Littorios as their objectives. One aircraft—one of those the Eagle had sent over—failed to return. Another was hit and momentarily put out of control as the pilot dived to the attack, but he recovered in time to launch his torpedo. He was again hit in the wing during the get-away but regained the carrier. By 2.50 a.m. on 12th November they were all back on board the Illustrious and the force was heading south to rejoin the Commander-in-Chief.

Meanwhile, the light forces in the Straits of Otranto had sighted in the bright moonlight a convoy of four merchantmen escorted by a destroyer and a torpedo boat, steering in the direction of Brindisi. Admiral Pridham-Wippell's force crept upon them unobserved. At 1.25 a.m. on 12th November, Commander J. W. Eaton in the Mohawk opened fire on the torpedo boat. The cruisers Orion, Sydney and Ajax and the destroyer Nubian dealt with the merchant ships. One was sunk, and two were set on fire and left sinking; the fourth escaped under cover of smoke. Their escort adopted the curious defence tactics of making off at full speed, and were not seen again. The raiders rejoined the Fleet at 11 a.m. "I trust," signalled the Commander-in-Chief, when they came within visual signalling distance, " you had many opportunities of using your heavy mashie," to which the Vice-Admiral, a naval golf champion, replied in a detailed affirmative.

By this time a photographic recon-naissance flight of R.A.F. aircraft from Malta had visited Taranto to count the spoils of the night's enterprise. These were subsequently confirmed as one Cavour and one Duilio-class battleship heavily damaged and beached and one Littorio-class battleship damaged. Half the Italian battle fleet had been crippled by eleven aircraft torpedoes.

On rejoining the Fleet, Rear-Admiral Lyster was greeted by a flag signal flying from the Warspite, the Commander-in-Chief's flagship: " Illustrious manœuvre well executed." It was the laconic understate-ment of a leader who knew the inadequacy of words. The night's work had made him master of the Mediterranean.

7. Malta Rides the Storm

T H E   P H A S E we have now reached in the naval war seems to present an opportune moment to record something of the ordeal through which Malta had passed since the entry of Italy into the war.

The policy governing the defence of Malta was based largely upon our alliance with France. With a powerful air and naval base at Bizerta, the threat to Malta of being bombed by Italy was discounted by the prac-ticability of immediate reprisals upon Sicilian and Italian cities. Reasonable men in those remote pre-war days argued perhaps that the mere possibility of such reprisals sufficed to protect civilians—at all events—from the in-humanities of aerial bombing. That France could collapse and make a separate peace was too fantastic a flight of imagination to con-template; and when almost without warning the incredible became an appalling fact, Malta was sadly short of its full means of defence.

Malta, with the little neighbouring island of Gozo, has an area of 117 square miles and a population of 275,000—it is the most densely populated area in Europe. This civil popu-lation suddenly became the largest internal commitment a fortress has had to accept in history. The Island's agricultural re-sources sufficed to feed one-third of the in-habitants. The rest—arms, equipment, fuel, petrol, food for the inhabitants and garrison —could only reach the island from the east. What the United Kingdom sent had virtually to circumnavigate Africa before it got there, fighting the Battle of the Atlantic on the way.

The people of Malta are believed to be of Phoenician descent. From the dawn of his-tory waves of conquest have swept over them or broken against their sandstone battle-ments. Sieges are in their blood. But in 1814 they asked leave to fly the British flag over the Island and perhaps thought that in so doing they had done with sieges.

Incorporated in the British Empire, Malta became the headquarters of the Fleet in the Mediterranean, and ever since there has been a peculiar bond between the Navy and the Maltese; for a century the Maltese have helped to man the Fleet. There has always been among the people on the one hand the innate devotion of the Maltese to the man he serves of his free will, and on the other the good-humoured affection of the British sailor for anybody who looks to him for defence or livelihood; and so it seemed somehow inevit-able that in the hour of Malta's extreme peril the Navy should take a large share of the

" FROM THE DAWN OF HISTORY waves of conquest have broken against their sandstone battlements.   Sieges are in their blood."   This is Valetta, Malta's capital, in a heavy air attack.

responsibility.   Lieut.-General Sir William Dobbie was the Governor.

The Flag Officer in Charge, Vice-Admiral Sir Wilbraham Ford, called for volunteers from dockyard workers to help man the defences.   They had no equipment, but they manned and fought the guns in overalls and carpet slippers.   The old tunnels, hewn by galley slaves to link the fortifications and the palaces, gave shelter from bombs to thousands of the inhabitants of Valetta, but they were not enough.   The Admiral set the dockyard forges to making picks by the thousand and served them out to an army of volunteer miners who attacked the soft sandstone and burrowed into it like badgers.   An Engineer Captain took over the problem of transport and petrol control for the Government, the Fighting Services and a quarter of a million inhabitants.   A Paymaster Captain grappled with the control of building materials and quarries for defence works.   An Australian

Paymaster Commander and the Naval Store Officer co-ordinated all supplies for the Island, and a Commander ran the shipping—ships that were, perhaps, loaded in British ports during a bombing raid, loaded and put to sea as fast as the stevedores could rush the stuff on board between " All Clear " and the next warning, and unloaded under much the same conditions.

The Government evolved an elaborate evacuation scheme for the densely populated cities adjoining the dockyard—Vittoriosa, Senglea and Cospicua.   The people were allocated by families to addresses in country districts, transport was organised on a huge scale, and all was ready for the exodus.   But the Maltese is a conservative being and of great independence of spirit.   The inhabitants of the death-traps of Vittoriosa, Senglea and Cospicua looked at the names and addresses of their compulsory hosts and what they said in effect was: " We don't think we know

the so-and-so's. No doubt they are very pleasant people, but we wonder if we should get on together. So in the circumstances perhaps it would be as well if we stayed where we are." The scheme collapsed.

When the raids began, however, and death and destruction rained down from Italian bombers upon Vittoriosa, Senglea and Cospicua (the parish priest of Senglea paced the main street at the height of the raids reading his office, to calm and fortify his flock) eighty thousand of the inhabitants rose up and evacuated themselves to friends and relations of their own choosing. They did it in twenty-four hours without panic or confusion; and it is said that wherever they went, crowding into the tiny stone cottages already full almost to capacity in the scorching heat of Malta's summer, they were received in the name of Christ the Compassionate by their friends; moreover there is no recorded instance of profiteering, or of advantage being taken of

them in their plight. In this fashion Malta " took it."

The Royal Malta Artillery and the King's Own Malta Regiment played the chief part in coastal and air defence at the outset and continue to provide about half the personnel of the Island's batteries. In addition, the monitor Terror had not long before reached Malta from the east, and her guns constituted a valuable addition to the defence of the Island. But guns alone are insufficient to defend a fortress against bombing. Fighters are needed, and, as has been noted earlier, there were no fighters on the Island at the outbreak of war. There were, however, in crates in a dockyard store, four sea-Gladiators awaiting shipment to the aircraft-carrier Eagle at Alexandria.

The Royal Air Force had on the Island a small force of practically obsolete London flying boats. The pilots of these boats had never flown a fighter machine in their lives; but the four of them took on the defence of Malta. They uncrated and assembled the Gladiators, and they flew them in combat with all that Italy chose to send against them. Wave after wave of bombers swept over the Island. They fought all day, coming down only to refuel and reammunition, taking on unimaginable odds. One machine was shot down, but the other three battled on in this fashion for two breath-taking months, when a squadron of Hurricanes came to their relief from England. Never before in its long history of assault had Malta seen so undaunted a defence: the inhabitants, peering out from the caves and tunnels at the three of them as they swooped against flights of ten, twenty and even fifty of the enemy, named them Faith, Hope and Charity.

That was the turn of the tide, and gradually Malta was built up again into as formidable a fortress as her strategic importance requires. Her garrison and people now number air raids by the thousand, but they keep stout hearts over the business. It is their tradition. In the great siege of 1565 a third

"ALL THAT ITALY CHOSE TO SEND." Here are Cant aircraft, surrounded by black shell-bursts, dropping their bombs. For two months, four R.A.F. flying-boat pilots, who had never flown a fighter, defended Malta with a Sea Gladiator apiece. Then the Hurricanes came.

THE LAST VISIT. The three burnt-out engines of an Italian bomber, which lies wrecked on one of Malta's fields.

of the population perished, but they saved Europe from the Turks; and every time her guns or fighters send the raiding bomber crashing down to mingle with the debris of her palaces and churches, it is all the yesterdays of Malta that light for her assailants " the way to dusty death."

8. Mussolini Mastered

O N E O F the immediate sequels to the crippling of Italy's battle fleet was the passage of a convoy through the Mediterranean from Gibraltar, carrying much-needed stores and equipment for Malta and Alexandria. These ships were escorted by the cruisers Manchester and Southampton. The Manchester was wearing the flag of Rear-Admiral L. E. Holland, and both cruisers carried military and R.A.F. reinforcements for Alexandria. As long as they were west of Malta, convoy and escort were covered by Admiral Somerville's Force H.

As usual, this main operation, requiring the Commander-in-Chief to be at sea with his Fleet in the central Mediterranean, was made the occasion for a number of subsidiary movements, aggressive and otherwise. The reduction in Italy's battle fleet enabled the Commander-in-Chief to dispense with two of his battleships for service elsewhere, and this opportunity was taken to pass the Ramillies and the cruisers Berwick and Newcastle westward. The other battleship, the Malaya, followed later. There were the usual inward and outward Malta convoys to be covered, and what had by now developed into a steady flow of reinforcements of men and material for Crete and Greece. Four corvettes, with the names of flowers, came to reinforce the Fleet under cover of the main convoy.

This multiplicity of comparatively slow movements across the length of the Mediterranean was in effect an almost triumphant assertion of sea power that we had never relinquished. While they were in progress the Illustrious carried out a raid on the Dodecanese, almost at the same moment that the Eagle had her bombers over Tripoli. These two gallant attacks by the Fleet Air Arm, 750 miles apart, were accomplished on the night of 25th November.

Admiral Holland and his cruisers were off Cape Spartivento in Sardinia on the morning of 27th when two enemy battleships and a cruiser force were reported at sea to the northward of him.

The Ramillies and her two cruiser consorts were then through the narrows on their way west. Admiral Somerville in the Renown, with the Sheffield and a valuable convoy under his wing, was coming east, and for a while the enemy was in a position to prevent the two from joining forces. For their own no doubt sufficient reasons the Italians turned away, pursued by our cruisers until the lengthening range made pursuit fruitless.

Admiral Somerville reinforced Admiral Holland's force, which was to the north of him, with the Sheffield and later with the Berwick and the Newcastle. The squadron of cruisers thus found itself assembled together under its Admiral for the first time. Its units had come from Iceland, the United Kingdom, the Azores, Gibraltar and China, to open fire simultaneously on a fleeing enemy.

The convoy passed safely through the narrows south of Sicily into the safe-guarding of the 1st Battle Squadron—acting in two Divisions—under the Commander-in-Chief. The Battle Squadron had been jealously " listening-in " to Force H's action with the enemy they had almost come to look upon as their exclusive prey. The Commander-in-Chief returned to Alexandria on 30th

November, the whole complicated operation having been brought to its conclusion without a hitch or casualty, except for the loss by the Illustrious of one of her Swordfish when bombing the Dodecanese.

By the end of the first week in December, it was evident that the Italian invasion of Greece had resulted in a serious defeat for the aggressors. They were plainly no match for the stout-hearted and inspired defenders of outraged liberties. The Italian Commander-in-Chief, Marshal Badoglio, resigned; the victor of Abyssinia had no stomach for this business; his naval confrère, Admiral Cavagnari, followed suit.

Rumours of their countrymen's prowess which reached the invaders of Egypt entrenched at Sidi Barrani, did nothing to whet their ardour to advance. On the night of 7th December any indecision they may have had in the matter was settled for them; the Army of the Nile swept forward in a surprise offensive and attacked at dawn over a wide front.

In anticipation of this advance, first fruits of British supremacy afloat, the shallow-draught monitor Terror, Commander H. J. Haynes, had been brought south from Crete. She led the little Aphis and the Ladybird and a more recent arrival, the Gnat, inshore off Sidi Barrani where, moving along the flank of the retreating Italians and supported by Fleet Air Arm spotting aircraft, they kept up a steady bombardment of the enemy's dust-veiled columns and transport. With interruptions caused by gales and sand-storms, merchant ships and small craft from Alexandria were employed in landing stores and water for the advancing army and its prisoners at successive points as they were abandoned by the enemy. All available space in these ships was used on the return journeys to relieve the army of the embarrassment of its hordes of prisoners ; by the middle of December there were thirty thousand of them.

These movements were covered by de·

stroyers of the Royal Australian Navy, and the whole force operating along the Libyan coast became known as the Inshore Squadron.

The enemy presumably did what they could to relieve the harassment of their retreating army. The Terror was attacked by E-boats which were driven off without achieving anything. Both she and the gunboats were constantly assailed by bombing and by torpedo-carrying aircraft, and occasionally they were shelled by shore artillery, but they came through unscathed. An

Italian submarine that poked her nose into these inshore operations was immediately sunk by destroyers.

As a result of the raid by the Illustrious on Taranto, the undamaged portion of the Italian battle fleet was transferred to Naples; here it was attacked by squadrons of R.A.F. Wellington bombers based on Malta. They also bombed the damaged battleship that had got no farther than the dock at Taranto.

December was a period of incessant activity afloat, which the enemy fleet seemed content to contemplate from its harbours. A large

ONE DAY'S WORK AT SEA. Following the swoop on Taranto, Britain was able to assert her sea-power throughout the length of the Mediterranean. This map shows something of the complex planning the exercise of sea-power entails. All the operations shown were in progress on one day, the 27th November, 1940. As a sequel to the

fleet operation similar to the previous one, covering convoys to and from Malta and up and down the Aegean, was accompanied by Fleet Air Arm attacks on the Dodecanese, on an Italian south-bound convoy from Sicily, when Swordfish sank 9,000 tons of shipping, and on Tripoli, where serious damage was caused to the port and shipping. The submarine Truant torpedoed and sank two supply ships and a tanker.

This period reached its climax with a sweep into the Adriatic by Admiral Pridham-Wippell's light forces and the bombardment of Valona in Albania by the Fleet flagship and the Valiant. On the calm and moonlit night of 18th December the two battleships poured an unexpected deluge of high-explosive—over a hundred 15-in. shells—into the Italian focus of supplies and troops operating against Greece. There has been nothing comparable to this phase of the war in the Mediterranean since Drake ranged the Spanish Main. Our forces withdrew without meeting any opposition, and the Commander-in-Chief took the opportunity to visit Malta for the first time since he left it with the Fleet

crippling of Italy's battle fleet sixteen days earlier, several powerful units are steaming west, released for duty elsewhere; convoys are going to and fro, escorted by destroyers and covered by Cruiser or Battle Squadrons, raids are being carried out on Italian bases and many other movements are taking place, all interdependent and exactly timed.

HAND IN HAND WITH THE ARMY. The Navy co-operates in General Wavell's advance into Libya in December, 1940. A tender, under cover of the Inshore Squadron, lands supplies on Sidi Barrani beach.

RANGED ON THE SHORE BATTERIES, the 15-inch guns of the shallow-draught monitor Terror help to reduce Bardia, where a strong Italian force was temporarily checking the British advance.

in May. The news of his intended arrival spread over the Island, and the Warspite entered the Grand Harbour to find every roof-top and point of vantage black with wildly cheering Maltese. The Fleet returned to Alexandria on Christmas Eve, having accomplished the last large-scale operation of the year. There was only one casualty, the destroyer Hyperion, which was mined while screening the Malaya and a west-bound convoy through the narrows. She was taken in tow by a sister destroyer, the Ilex, but the approaching dawn found them dangerously close to the island of Pantellaria, and she was abandoned and sunk by order of the Commander-in-Chief. About that time the Greek Navy showed its fighting qualities by conducting a destroyer sweep into the Adriatic, while a Greek submarine, the Papanikolis, sank three large enemy troopships and another, the Katsonis, drove a tanker ashore and set her ablaze.

The Army of the Nile, supported by the R.A.F. who, although preposterously outnumbered, stubbornly maintained their ascendancy in the air, continued to thrust the

Italians westward. Sidi Barrani and Buq Buq, Sollum and Fort Capuzzo, were occupied in turn. A force of about 20,000 Italians finally made a stand at Bardia, where they were invested.

Creeping from inlet to inlet along the coast the Aphis reached the harbour of Bardia unobserved in the dawn of 17th December. Entering, she set three ships on fire at a range of 600 yards and then turned her attention to the entrenched Italians in the wadi ashore. The Terror, brooding over her bantling from seaward, while she ranged on the shore batteries, observed " volumes of black smoke rolling out of the entrance of the harbour " and reported that the Aphis " appeared to be having a good time."

The Aphis, under heavy Breda, rifle and machine-gun fire, repeatedly hit, but without casualties, withdrew after twenty minutes of this gallant and impertinent attack. Her Captain, Lieutenant-Commander J. O. Campbell, remarked nonchalantly to the Terror that the " noise value " of his 6-in. bombardment must have been enormous, as he counted four echoes when the first round

THE LAST PHASE AT BARDIA. On 17th December, the little gunboat Aphis slipped unobserved into Bardia's narrow harbour and wrecked all these ships with her 6-inch guns. Repeatedly hit, she withdrew without casualties.

5th January all resistance ceased. Forty-five thousand officers and men had been killed or captured, our casualties being in the region of four hundred.

The effects of the sober and reasoned appeal to the Italian people made by the Prime Minister of Great Britain, the military reverses in Albania and Libya and the reluctance of the Italian fleet to seek an issue in what Mussolini liked to describe as *Mare nostrum*, made his need for help imperative. Nothing much could be done to stiffen the arm of the Italian navy but, in response to the jackal's dismal howl, sections of the German air force were moved into Italy. The baleful symbol of the swastika was about to appear in the skies of the Mediterranean.

was fired, and altogether he fired a hundred!

The Italian resistance at Bardia checked the main advance but did not entirely hold it. To demoralise and dislodge a force of this size, entrenched as it was, a greater weight of metal was required than the Terror and the gunboats could hurl into its defences. On 3rd January, 1941, the Battle Fleet took a hand in support of the final assault by the army. The Fleet flagship and two other battleships, protected during daylight from air attack by fighters from the Illustrious, and screened by destroyers, steamed to and fro off the coast delivering a devastating 15-in. bombardment. Their Swordfish, catapulted off before the guns opened fire, spotted the fall of shot. A most gallantly served shore battery stood up to this shelling for a while and came very near hitting the flagship; it continued to bark defiance as long as the Fleet was in range.

It was one of the rare occasions in history when the fire of a battle fleet has been concentrated on an area surrounded on three sides by our troops. Materially and morally the results were catastrophic. By midday on

9. Enter the Luftwaffe:

the Illustrious Comes Through

By JANUARY, 1941, the vital necessity confronting the Commander-in-Chief was to get supplies, reinforcements and equipment to the aid of Greece.

Early in the month another of the large-scale operations took place in co-operation with Force H, to cover an important convoy of ships bound for Malta and the Piraeus. On 10th, when the convoy was to the south of Sicily, two of the escorting cruisers, the Bonaventure, commanded by Captain H. J. Egerton, and the Southampton, commanded by Captain B. C. B. Brooke, sighted two enemy destroyers. It was just getting light and the enemy had probably stumbled on the convoy inadvertently; on form, it is unlikely to have been a deliberate attempt to intercept it. In the ensuing engagement one destroyer was blown up and the other escaped at high speed.

The Commander-in-Chief with the main Fleet was to the eastward of this action, and seeing the gun-flashes, closed towards them. A few minutes later, one of the screening destroyers, the Gallant, struck a mine which blew her bows off. The Bonaventure stood by while Commander J. W. Eaton took her in tow with the Mohawk. Rear-Admiral E. de F. Renouf then arrived with his cruisers Gloucester and Southampton to cover the tow and beat off intermittent bombing attacks.

In the meanwhile, at about 9.30 a.m., the Fleet had been located by an enemy shadower, which was shot down by Fulmars patrolling from the Illustrious. Three hours later two S.79s dived in at the Valiant out of high clouds and dropped torpedoes, which missed. They made off pursued by the Fulmars.

The Fleet was then about 100 miles to the westward of Malta, with the convoy and its escort away to the southward; at 12.35 a large formation of probably forty to fifty Ju.87s and 88s appeared, approaching from the north, and made a dive-bombing attack on the Fleet. Apart from the markings on the wings, the technical skill and fanatical determination with which the attack was delivered showed that there was a new factor to be dealt with in the Mediterranean war. Both in numbers and performance this attack surpassed anything yet experienced.

The Illustrious was actually flying off a squadron of relief Fulmar and Swordfish patrollers when the Junkers were sighted. She got them safely off, and then appeared to vanish from sight in a great cliff of spray and water thrown up from the placid sea by bursting bombs. It was plain that she had been singled out as the main target of the attack. When she reappeared she had hauled out of line, grievously stricken and heavily on fire. Although not under control, with her flight deck wrecked, she con-

trived to beat off another savage attack with her guns.

In some miraculous fashion she managed by 3.30 p.m. to effect sufficient temporary repairs to enable her to head for Malta, steering by her main engines. Those of her Fulmars that had gone in pursuit of the S.79s, got back too late to intervene before the first attack, and those flown off to relieve them could not attain effective height in time. However, they shot down eight during this and subsequent attacks, coming down at Malta for fuel and ammunition at intervals as they fought the enemy throughout the day.

Captain D. W. Boyd, steering only with the propellers, and with fires still burning, got his ship into harbour at Malta after dark, having beaten off five more attacks on the way and been hit again. The Illustrious was berthed alongside the dockyard, disembarked her dead and wounded, and finally extinguished the last fire, having accomplished, under heavy punishment and partly disabled, a six hours' journey in perilous daylight.

In the following dawn the Gallant arrived minus her bows, having been towed 120 miles by the Mohawk with only the foremost bulkhead standing between salvation and total loss. This remarkable feat accomplished, and having seen the Gallant safely into harbour, the Mohawk and her cruiser escort hastened to rejoin the Fleet.

The crippling of the Illustrious temporarily deprived the Fleet of its essential air support, and was a decided setback; another was in store. At 3 p.m. on 11th January, Rear-Admiral Renouf in the Gloucester, overtaking the Fleet after escorting the Mohawk and the Gallant to Malta, reported that the Southampton and the Gloucester had been attacked by twelve dive-bombers out of the sun, and both ships had been hit. The Southampton struggled on for an hour and then stopped. Fires completely out of control were raging over the after engine-room and one of the magazines. At 9 p.m. the Commander-in-Chief ordered her to be

THE ORDEAL OF THE ILLUSTRIOUS. *Above*, German dive-bombers begin their attack at 12.35 p.m. on 10th January, 1941. The Illustrious is with the Fleet, a hundred miles west of Malta. *Below*, she is badly damaged and set on fire, but six hours later she reached Malta.

THE FIGHT FOR HER LIFE. The Illustrious's ordeal was not yet at an end. *Below*, she lies alongside the dockyard at Malta, a motionless target for repeated dive-bombing attacks, while working parties labour to repair her damage. On 23rd January she slipped out and reached Alexandria under her own steam.

abandoned and sunk. Her officers and men were transferred to the Gloucester and one of the destroyer screen, the Diamond, which rejoined the Fleet.

The convoy that had been the main object of the operation reached Malta and Greece safely and the Fleet returned to Alexandria. Greece had been strengthened and Malta and its guns fed, but the price had been high.

It was now the turn of Malta, harbouring the crippled Illustrious and Gallant, and unloading the newly arrived convoy ships, to endure the fury of the dive-bombers. The dockyard was heavily raided on 16th

THE SHIP LIVES. After further repairs at Alexandria, the Illustrious sailed for the United States, where she was restored and made fit for service again.

January and the Illustrious was again hit, but not seriously damaged. One of the ships of the recently arrived convoy, however, was not so fortunate. Her engine-room was wrecked, with thirty-eight casualties, though her cargo, 4,000 tons of ammunition, was not damaged.

The story of the Merchant Navy throughout the war in the Mediterranean is one of unostentatious gallantry and hardihood. From the time they entered the narrow seas until they left them—usually to return again and again in fresh convoys—these ships were liable to ceaseless attack at sea and in harbour. Those unloading at Malta were, in the words of one shipwrecked there before them, in jeopardy every hour. The Navy shared the perils with them, and in turn the Merchant Navy shared with the Fleet the same confidence in ultimate victory, the same selfless devotion to duty.

Malta was once more savagely bombed on 18th January, and again next day, when the Illustrious was once more damaged. During these raids over forty enemy aircraft were shot down, but they did not cease coming over; in all, the island was raided fifty-eight times during the month. Most of these raids were directed against the Illustrious, undergoing repair alongside the dockyard. Not only were her guns manned day and night, but they were almost ceaselessly in action. Volunteers—officers, petty officers and ableseamen—fought them while the devoted artizans and artificers and working parties laboured below to repair her. In spite of these daunting conditions they contrived with the help of the dockyard to patch her up sufficiently for the voyage.

During a lull between raids on the night of 23rd January the Illustrious slipped out and was escorted to Alexandria under her own steam, covered by the Fleet. She arrived with a bare 60 tons of oil fuel left on board, and was greeted by the cheers of every ship in harbour. She escaped further attack during the passage, but the escorting cruiser squadron was heavily though unsuccessfully attacked by high-level and dive-bombers.

It is probable that the Germans, who do not do things by halves, had sent four or five hundred bombers to Sicily and North Africa. At least a quarter of these were destroyed in action or on the ground in our counter-bombing raids from Malta. A squadron of Swordfish was already operating there. The Illustrious's Fulmars joined the R.A.F. defence squadrons and her remaining Swordfish were divided between Crete and the Western Desert.

In the western basin of the Mediterranean, Admiral Somerville's hands were free just then to hit back in no uncertain fashion. Torpedo-carrying aircraft from the Ark Royal attacked the dam at Lake Tirso in Sardinia on 1st February and on the 9th the whole of Force H bombarded Genoa. Over 1,300 shells of calibres varying from 15 in. to 4·5 in. were fired into docks and workshops with results which Admiral Somerville described as " excellent." The Ark Royal's aircraft bombed Leghorn and Pisa at the same time.

10. The Little Ships Along the Coast

THE ARMY OF THE NILE continued its triumphant advance westward. Tobruk fell on 22nd January after a bombardment by the Terror and the gunboats. The Italian cruiser San Giorgio, inside the harbour, was bombed by the R.A.F. and destroyed by the Italians. Derna was occupied on 30th January and Benghazi surrendered during the night of 6th February; our troops swept on to El Agheila.

The rapidly lengthening lines of communication in Libya, however, made heavy demands on the Inshore Squadron. Not only had it to keep pace with the Army's requirements, but tens of thousands of prisoners had to be transported back to Alexandria—not only transported, but provided with food, water and medical attention. Far away over the sky-line the Imperial forces were exploiting their success with brilliant energy, looking to the Inshore Squadron somehow to provide the next meal. That the latter was always forthcoming must have given it the miraculous property of manna. It never failed because, in spite of the dive-bombers, the Inshore Squadron had the British Battle Fleet behind it. Such is the special and vital quality of sea power.

Reinforcements for the Army were sent forward when and how ships could take them. Large numbers of military passengers penned between decks in little ships during the bad weather prevalent at this time of year, called from one destroyer petty officer the devout comment: " Well, all I can say is, thank God them soldiers don't bring their ruddy horses with them! "

Gales and sand-storms continued to hamper operations; the newly acquired harbours, Tobruk, Derna and Benghazi, were blocked with the wreckage of sunken ships, their quays and landing facilities in ruins, their breakwaters breached by shell-fire and bombing.

But far worse than these difficulties were the ceaseless attacks from the German bombers and aircraft minelayers. The newly acquired airfields along the coast gave little security; the outnumbered air force had its work cut out to maintain pressure on the retreating enemy, and no fighters to spare for the defence of coastwise shipping. The Swordfish squadron from the Illustrious, after operating in the desert for a few weeks, had to be transferred to Crete to meet a new threat from the air developing in the Dodecanese against the Suez Canal.

On 9th February the Commander-in-Chief made the following signal to the Inshore Squadron:

> The feat of the Army in clearing Egypt and occupying Cyrenaica in a period of eight weeks is an outstanding achievement to which the Inshore Squadron and the shore parties along the coast have contributed in no small measure. I am fully alive to the fact that this result has been made possible by an unbreakable determination to allow no obstacle to stand in the way of meeting all requirements. All officers and men who took part in these operations may well feel proud, as I do, of their contribution to this victory.

The dropping of magnetic and acoustic mines by aircraft assumed ugly proportions. Not only were the Libyan harbours the object of nightly visitations, but Malta harbour and the Suez Canal were fouled by German aircraft from Sicily and Rhodes. Until adequate mine-sweeping forces arrived, the situation was serious. For a time the eastern entrance to the Mediterranean was blocked; and without a modern aircraft-carrier to support the Fleet it was not possible to bring convoys through the Mediterranean from the west.

Reinforcements of minesweepers fitted to deal with both magnetic and acoustic mines were sent up from South Africa, and the Canal was fully opened by the middle of March, which not only enabled the Illustrious to be moved away for extensive repair, but admitted her sister carrier, the Formidable, into the Mediterranean. The Fleet again had the " umbrella " of its air-arm.

The dive-bombers took heavy toll of the Inshore Squadron. The minesweeper Huntley on her way to Derna was bombed and machine-gunned and, fighting back with every available weapon, was finally sunk by aircraft torpedoes. The hospital ship Dorsetshire, though fully illuminated, was bombed and near-missed in the Gulf of Sollum. The destroyer Dainty, whose Captain, Commander M. S. Thomas, had bagged three submarines in two successive days in June, and which had a record of duty invariably well and bravely done, was dive-bombed and sunk off Tobruk. A month before she had earned a signal of congratulations from the Commander-in-Chief for towing a torpedoed tanker into Suda Bay. On her first night with the Inshore Squadron she captured two Italian schooners, the Tiberio and the Maria Giovanna, which were later destined, as units of the Royal Navy, to play a notable part in sustaining Tobruk.

The trawler Ouse and the South African whaler Southern Floe fell victims to mines, and at last the Terror went. In a dawn raid on Benghazi on 22nd February she received a near miss which started slow flooding of several compartments. Aware that the Luftwaffe were bent on her destruction, Commander Haynes, asking for fighter protection which could not be afforded, stoically concluded his signal, " I consider it only a matter of time before the ship receives a direct hit."

She sailed at dusk for Tobruk and two mines that exploded near her caused further flooding of her compartments. The next day she was again dive-bombed and this time her engine-room was flooded and her back broken. But the spirit of her officers and men was not to be broken. She still struggled gallantly eastward in an attempt to make Derna, with the minesweeper Fareham and the corvette Salvia trying to take her in tow. She was abandoned at 2 a.m. on 25th February, with a heavy list to starboard, and finally sank two hours later.

She was a veteran of the Belgian coast in the last war; she had defended Malta and Suda Bay against severe air attacks when no other defence was available. For two months her squat form had wallowed through gales and sand-storms in offensive bombardments off the Libyan coast, while she covered with her 15-in. guns her venturesome brood of gunboats in their assaults. The rifling of her guns grew so worn that the ton-weight

IN THE WESTERN DESERT: THE NAVY'S PART. *Left*, fires raging in Tobruk after the naval bombardment which preceded the fall of the stronghold to General Wavell on 22nd January, 1941. In the harbour can be seen the half-sunk Italian cruiser San Giorgio. *Right*, small craft of the Inshore Squadron help the Eighth Army by evacuating thousands of Italian prisoners.

projectiles somersaulted about the enemy encampments like skittles in a bowling alley, before they finally exploded. She had been a sort of Universal Aunt to the advancing army, acting as water carrier, supply vessel and repair ship. In the swiftly occupied harbours where all was improvisation, hers was the only effective defence against the Luftwaffe. Let it be her epitaph that she had endured all things and done well.

On 4th March, 1941, the Commander-in-Chief was promoted to be a Knight Grand Cross of the Most Honourable Order of the Bath. " I would rather," he said when told of it, his mind on the little ships he had to send continuously along that dive-bombed coast, " I would rather they had given me three squadrons of Hurricanes."

Our victories in Libya, and the mauling the Italian armies had received from the Greeks, made it plain to the senior partner of the Axis that Germany must intervene in the Mediterranean with more than dive-bombers if Italy was not to crack from end to end. Concentrations of mechanised troops in Italian ports pointed to a German thrust into Libya through Tripoli; armoured divisions massing in Bulgaria and on the borders of

Yugoslavia boded an assault of overwhelming strength on Greece or Turkey.

The decision to help Greece with all means at our disposal meant calling a halt to the victorious Libyan offensive, and the withdrawal of a large proportion of the Army of the Nile. It was virtually a surrender of Libya to enable us to keep our promise to Greece, and if future historians ever need an example of how Britain honours her plighted word, they have it here. By comparison with Italian losses in North Africa ours had been almost insignificant. But if blood must be the price of a pledge between nations, then the Navy was destined later to pay it in full measure.

As the first weeks of March passed and the commencement of hostilities by Germany grew more imminent, the operation of transporting the Army into Greece became a rush against time. The passage from Egyptian ports to the Piraeus, virtually the only port in the country, led past the chain of enemy bases in the Dodecanese. From these his air and sea forces were in ideal positions to operate against our lines of communication. This made heavy demands on our destroyers; even the Inshore Squadron had to be deprived of its destroyers to furnish escorts for the Aegean convoys. Besides this, there was always the threat of raids by heavy surface forces from Taranto and Messina. As will be seen, one of these actually materialised and became the Battle of Matapan.

To meet this particular menace it was necessary to keep a force of cruisers—who were perpetually dive-bombed—constantly patrolling to the west of Crete and in the Aegean. They used Suda Bay in Crete as a fuelling base, and it was here that the cruiser York was torpedoed on 25th March by a one-man fast-planing dinghy that penetrated the defences. The Bonaventure, torpedoed on 31st March, when covering a convoy returning from the Aegean, was another casualty resulting from these operations. But the Navy fulfilled its obligation to the Army. Out of the entire force ultimately transported, not a single man, gun or vehicle was lost in transit.

11. The Enemy is Brought to Battle

Be pleased to lay before Their Lordships the attached reports of the Battle of Matapan, 27–30 March, 1941. Five ships of the enemy fleet were sunk, burned or destroyed as per margin. Except for the loss of one aircraft in action, our fleet suffered no damage or casualties.
Commander-in-Chief's dispatch.

T O W A R D S T H E E N D of March there were indications that the enemy was beginning to display increasing interest in the activities of the British Fleet in the eastern Mediterranean. Reconnaissance aircraft quartered the skies to the south and west of Greece and dogged the Aegean convoys: there were almost daily attempts to reconnoitre Alexandria harbour.

These evidences of intensified curiosity, and the imminence of the German attack on Greece, suggested to the Commander-in-Chief the possibility that a large-scale operation was contemplated, the nature of which he could not foretell. He had to weigh in his mind the relative likelihoods of an attack on our convoys in the Aegean, of an enemy convoy being escorted to the Dodecanese, of a landing in Cyrenaica or of one in Greece. There was even the possibility of an assault on Malta. Any one of these eventualities would call for completely different dispositions of his forces. Had he taken the Fleet into the central Mediterranean and waited on events, nothing would have happened until he was obliged to return to harbour for fuel, when the enemy would have made a dash for whatever enterprise he was contemplating.

This is the riddle of the sphinx for ever confronting leaders in war—the interpretation of the enemy's intentions. But Admiral Cunningham's responsibility was two-fold: there was the Army to consider, part of which had to be victualled in Libya and the rest transported to Greece; and there was his own unwearying purpose of bringing the enemy fleet to action. If he guessed right, it might give him victory, but if he guessed wrong all would be very wrong: he had no margin for error.

At noon on 27th March three enemy cruisers and a destroyer were sighted by air reconnaissance 120 miles south-east from the toe of Italy, steering a south-easterly course. It was little enough on which to form a vital decision, but the Commander-in-Chief made it. At dusk on 27th he sailed the Fleet from Alexandria.

We have noted that the new aircraft-carrier Formidable, under command of Captain A. W. La T. Bisset, had now joined the Fleet in place of the crippled Illustrious. The Eagle had gone east through the Canal. Rear-Admiral Lyster had been appointed Fifth Sea Lord and Rear-Admiral D. W. Boyd, the late Captain of the Illustrious, had relieved him in Command of Aircraft Carriers in the Mediterranean.

He had established a Fleet Air Arm reserve fighter squadron (No. 805) at Maleme in Crete to provide coastal fighter protection for the Aegean and Suda Bay convoys. We have also seen that the Illustrious's Swordfish, after a few weeks in the desert, were also transferred to Crete; in March, however, this squadron (No. 815) split up and a part moved to Greece where it operated from Eleusis, near Athens, using Paramythia, on the mainland east of Corfu, as a forward base for attacking Durazzo, Valona and Brindisi. These squadrons and those in the Formidable played a most decisive part in subsequent events.

It would be well at this juncture to enumerate the British forces and their dispositions before they are alternately lost to view and emerge and are lost again in the tumultuous convolutions of a day and night fleet action.

The Commander-in-Chief led the Battle Fleet in the Warspite with the Barham, wearing the flag of Rear-Admiral H. B. Rawlings, commanding 1st Battle Squadron, the Valiant, and the Formidable, wearing the flag of the Rear-Admiral Aircraft Carriers. They were screened by the 14th Destroyer Flotilla, H.M.S. Jervis, Janus, Nubian and Mohawk and the 10th Flotilla, H.M.S. Stuart, Greyhound, Griffin, Hotspur and Havock.

The Second-in-Command, Vice-Admiral Pridham-Wippell, was ordered to rendezvous next morning south of Gavdhos Island, with the cruisers Orion, Ajax, Perth and Gloucester, and the 2nd Destroyer Flotilla, H.M.S. Ilex, Hasty, Vendetta and Hereward.

ITALIAN PRIDE AND POWER. Of these four fast 8-inch gun cruisers —the Zara, the Fiume, the Gorizia and the Pola—here shown lying snug in Naples harbour, three were soon to be destroyed in the Battle of Matapan.

The 2nd, 10th and 14th flotillas were commanded respectively by Captain H. St. L. Nicolson, Captain H. M. L. Waller, Royal Australian Navy, and Captain P. J. Mack.

Soon after dawn on 28th March, one of the Formidable's aircraft on reconnaissance reported three cruisers and four destroyers about thirty miles south of Gavdhos Island, steering south-south-east. This was somewhere in the neighbourhood of Admiral Pridham-Wippell's force, and at 7.45 a.m. he sighted them to the northward. They were a long way off, but he suspected them to be 8-in. gun ships, which the Second-in-Command knew could outrange his squadron and had superior speed. He decided, therefore, to turn to the south-east, feigning flight, and try to entice the enemy towards the Battle Fleet. It will be convenient to call this squadron of enemy cruisers Force X.

The ruse succeeded, and Force X followed for three-quarters of an hour, firing at inter-

THE DECOY. Feigning flight, and laying a smoke-screen, the cruiser Gloucester, with the Orion, the Ajax and the Perth, draws the Italian forces towards the British Battle Fleet. 15-inch shells from the Italian battleship Vittorio Veneto, which has suddenly appeared on the scene, fall near H.M.S. Gloucester.

vals, but keeping out of range, with the result that salvoes on both sides fell short. At 8.55 a.m. the enemy turned away to the north-west. He had previously catapulted an aircraft which probably reported the composition of our cruiser force, and he had in fact decided to reverse his tactics. Admiral Pridham-Wippell turned in pursuit and at 10.58 a.m. sighted a battleship to the northward, which opened an accurate fire on him from sixteen miles away as he turned back behind a smoke-screen. He was momentarily in an uncomfortable position, with a battleship on one quarter and Force X on the other, both with the range of him. To his relief the battleship suddenly ceased firing, but her reason for doing this was concealed by the smoke. Force X, also invisible from our cruisers for the same reason, was legging it for home.

At this point we must switch to the aircraft-carrier Formidable. Just before 10 a.m. the Commander-in-Chief ordered a striking-force of Albacores armed with torpedoes, escorted by a couple of Fulmars, to be flown off to deal with Force X; but on reaching the scene of action the pilots discovered that what had in fact been delivered into their hands was a Littorio battleship—it turned out later to be the Vittorio Veneto, the Italian flagship—escorted by four destroyers. She had just commenced heavy and accurate 15-in. gun fire on our cruisers, and the Albacores were just about in time.

Under the leadership of Lieutenant-Commander W. H. G. Saunt, they dived to attack through a desperate barrage and scored a hit aft which not only caused the Vittorio Veneto to break off the action against our cruisers, but had the effect of reducing her speed. She turned away to the westward. Two Junkers 88's that had started off to attack our cruisers were pursued by the Albacores' Fulmar escort. One Junkers was shot down and the other made off.

In the meanwhile, the only three Sword-fish at the Fleet Air Arm base at Maleme in

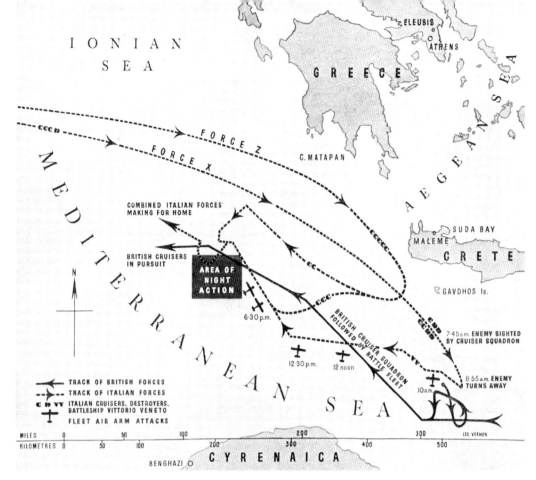

SKIRMISH BEFORE MATAPAN. Two separate squadrons of Italian cruisers and the battleship Vittorio Veneto were sighted by air reconnaissance west and south-west of Crete on the early morning of 28th March. British cruisers decoyed them towards the Battle Fleet, which had sailed the day before from Alexandria, but they turned for home before they could be brought to action. The Vittorio Veneto and other enemy ships were repeatedly hit by air attack and their speed reduced; when dusk came they were still in flight and still pursued by the Cruiser Squadron. There followed the night Battle of Matapan, when the British Battle Fleet, following up behind the cruisers, encountered part of the Italian fleet which had turned back to look for one of its casualties.

Crete had been armed with torpedoes and sent off to deal with Force X. They found them still retreating westward and attacked them out of a noon sun.

A new enemy force was now reported by a patrolling Sunderland as being some thirty-five miles to the westward of Gavdhos Island. This consisted of two Abruzzi-class cruisers and three Zara-class. Let us call it Force Z. It was steering to the north-westward and was about a hundred miles in that direction from the British Fleet. At 12.30, to the relief of the Commander-in-Chief, the Second-in-

Command appeared with all his force intact and rejoined the Fleet.

It was now apparent to the Commander-in-Chief, from reconnaissance aircraft reports, that his forces could not overtake the Vittorio Veneto and Force X, unless the speed of the former could be further reduced. He therefore ordered the Formidable to dispatch a second striking-force. This flew off under Lieutenant-Commander J. Dalyell-Stead at 12.30 p.m., and attacked the Vittorio Veneto out of the sun. She was hit by two, possibly more, torpedoes. The

Squadron Commander was last seen diving in to attack over one of the screening destroyers, and failed to return. The remainder landed on at 4 p.m.

At this juncture Force Z was about 120 miles north-west from the Commander-in-Chief, steering to the north-westward at 30 knots. Force X and the damaged Vittorio Veneto, whose speed was reduced to 13 knots as a result of the Fleet Air Arm attack, were 60 miles closer, but could not be overhauled by the Battle Fleet before dark. Admiral Pridham-Wippell was therefore sent on at full speed with his light forces to make contact. A third air striking-force was presently flown off to attack the Italian flagship at dusk.

The Swordfish carried by the Warspite was catapulted off at 5.45 p.m., and from the pilot's reports it appeared that the Vittorio Veneto was now doing 15 knots; to port of her were three 6-in. gun cruisers and on the starboard wing were three 8-in. gun cruisers—presumably from Force Z—the whole massed force screened by eleven destroyers. In addition to this party the other two cruisers in Force Z, the Abruzzi and the Garibaldi, were still somewhere to the north-west.

Soon after noon the Commander of 815 Squadron at Eleusis, Lieutenant F. M. A. Torrens-Spence, flew over to Maleme with the only serviceable Swordfish they had and their only torpedo; the rest of the Squadron at Maleme was by then also reduced to one Swordfish and torpedo. The two of them went off alone on the hazardous duty of attacking a battleship, six cruisers and eleven destroyers all very much on the alert. They arrived to find the Formidable's striking-force also manœuvring in the clouds for position to attack. One attached himself to this force, the other with some aloofness of spirit went off and attacked by himself. " As searchlights were being pointed in my direction," his report concludes, " I did not stay to observe results." The others, again led by Lieutenant-Commander Saunt, attacked from widely different angles through an appalling barrage of fire and searchlights. They all returned safely to Maleme, landing in darkness and uncertain what they had actually achieved. They were unaware that they had hit the Pola, which dropped out of line and eventually stopped.

It was now nearly dark. The Second-in-Command, pressing on in pursuit of the enemy, saw the sky ahead filled with spouts of coloured tracer ammunition and bursting shells; it was the Italian fleet's reaction to the torpedo air attack. " They must have been very gallant men," he commented in his despatch, " who went through it to get their torpedoes home." The firing died away with the last of the light. The British cruisers held on their course unaware that, after the attack, the enemy had turned to the south-west. The Second-in-Command never regained contact with them.

12. Night Victory off Matapan

T HE C O M M A N D E R - I N - C H I E F , in deciding to engage in a night action, had to accept certain risks. Apart from the powerful force screening his quarry, there was Force Z—two cruisers and five destroyers—somewhere in the darkness to the northward. On the other hand, the enemy were only 300 miles from home and by daylight would be under the cover of their dive-bombers. Admiral Cunningham could not afford to subject his fleet to air attack on such a scale. He therefore accepted the hazards involved in a battleship night action, and at 8.40 p.m. sent his destroyers in to the attack.

The necessity for providing protection for the vital Aegean convoys had reduced the number of destroyers available for fleet work to an absurdly small force, and only eight destroyers, in two divisions, formed the attacking force. The odds were dead against them, and they knew it. Captain Mack led them in the Jervis, with Captain Nicolson in the Ilex commanding the second division. The Commander-in-Chief retained Captain Waller, the Australian, in the Stuart, with the Havock, the Greyhound and the Griffin, to act as a screen to the Battle Fleet, and ordered the striking-force to proceed to where he believed the enemy to be. What at this point nobody appreciated, was the fact that the Italian cruiser Pola had stopped after being torpedoed by the Swordfish, that three cruisers and some destroyers had turned back to go to her support, and that the rest of the enemy force, after turning to the south-west for some distance, had turned again to the north-west.

At 10.25 p.m. two large cruisers and a smaller one were unexpectedly sighted by the Warspite steaming on an opposite course, about 2 miles away. Although they were clearly visible through night-glasses, it was apparent, though incredible, that they were serenely unconscious of the presence of the Battle Fleet. They had presumably turned back in search of the damaged Pola. The Greyhound, the screening destroyer nearest to them, switched her searchlight on to the second large cruiser in the line; the merciless glare revealed that her guns were trained fore and aft; every detail of her construction stood out vividly in the illumination of the Greyhound's questioning stare. Almost simultaneously the Warspite and the Valiant's 15-in. guns opened fire. The enemy ship was seen to be the Fiume. Both broadsides hit. She appeared to change into a sheet of flame that was only extinguished half an hour later when she sank.

The leading ship in the enemy line, as seen from the Barham, was silhouetted against the beam of the Greyhound's searchlight. Captain G. Cooke opened fire and hit her with the first broadside. She turned away to starboard, a dull glow of internal fires partly obscured by smoke. Her identity and subsequent fate are unknown. She was not seen again.

Captain C. E Morgan of the Valiant shifted his fire to the second ship in the line, now illuminated by searchlights and starshell. This was the Zara. Fire from all three battleships was concentrated on her at 3,000 yards range. She was hit by at least twenty 15-in. shells. The Jervis found her a burning hulk still floating at about 2.30 a.m. and sank her with a torpedo.

Meanwhile, in the terrible illumination of starshell, blazing ships and gun flashes, a number of enemy destroyers appeared astern of the Fiume and fired torpedoes at the battleships before making off to the westward. The leading destroyers were hit by 6-in. shell from the Warspite, as the Battle Fleet swung to starboard to avoid the torpedoes. The Commander-in-Chief, with the battleships and the Formidable, then withdrew to the north-eastward to avoid the possibility of being torpedoed, in the confusion of a destroyer *mêlée*, by his own forces. That a contretemps of this nature was already taking place in the ranks of Tuscany was indicated by starshell and heavy firing on a bearing that none of our ships had reached. The Vittorio Veneto is believed to have shelled one of her own cruisers in this action.

Before turning, the Commander-in-Chief launched his screening destroyers to the attack. The 10th Flotilla went off in pairs— the Stuart led the Havock towards the burning cruisers; the Greyhound and the Griffin went off after the fleeing destroyers.

Just before 11 p.m. the Stuart saw an enemy cruiser, probably the Zara, stationary and ablaze. Another, apparently undamaged, was circling her and solicitously making

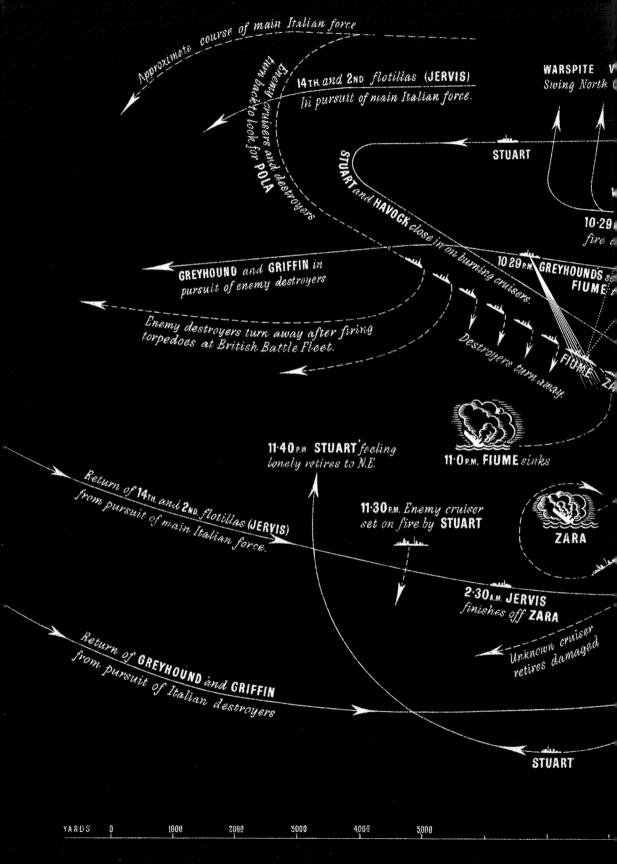

Approximate course of main Italian force

Enemy cruisers and destroyers turn back to look for POLA

14TH. **and 2**ND **flotillas (JERVIS)**
In pursuit of main Italian force.

WARSPITE V
Swing North C

STUART

STUART and **HAVOCK** close in on burning cruisers.

10·29

fire e

GREYHOUND and **GRIFFIN** in
pursuit of enemy destroyers

10·29 P.M. GREYHOUNDS se
FIUME

Enemy destroyers turn away after firing
torpedoes at British Battle Fleet.

Destroyers turn away.

FIUME

ZA

11·40 P.M **STUART** feeling
lonely retires to N.E.

11·0 P.M. **FIUME** sinks

11·30 P.M. Enemy cruiser
set on fire by **STUART**

Return of **14**TH. **and 2**ND. **flotillas (JERVIS)**
from pursuit of main Italian force.

ZARA

2·30 A.M. **JERVIS**
finishes off **ZARA**

Unknown cruiser
retires damaged

Return of **GREYHOUND** and **GRIFFIN**
from pursuit of Italian destroyers

STUART

YARDS   0   1000   2000   3000   4000   5000

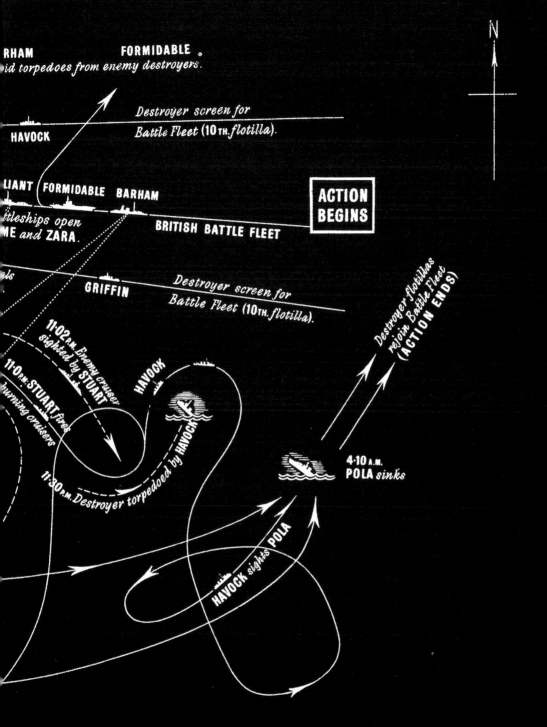

RHAM   FORMIDABLE

id torpedoes from enemy destroyers.

N

HAVOCK

Destroyer screen for
Battle Fleet (10 TH. *flotilla*).

LIANT | FORMIDABLE | BARHAM

tleships open
ME and ZARA.

BRITISH BATTLE FLEET

ACTION BEGINS

ds

GRIFFIN

Destroyer screen for
Battle Fleet (10TH. *flotilla*).

Destroyer flotillas
rejoin Battle Fleet
(ACTION ENDS)

11·02 P.M. *Enemy cruisers*
sighted by STUART

11·0 P.M. *STUART fires*

urning cruisers

HAVOCK

Destroyer torpedoed by HAVOCK

11·30 P.M.

4·10 A.M.
POLA *sinks*

HAVOCK *sights* POLA

MATAPAN, THE NIGHT ACTION: 28TH MARCH, 1941

10000   15,000   LEO·VERNON

signals. The Stuart, judging her moment, fired her full outfit of torpedoes at the pair of them. She also opened fire on the burning ship, which provoked brief response, followed by silence.

The Captain of the Stuart proceeded to turn his attention to her consort, who was found to be lying stopped 1,500 yards away, with a heavy list. At this moment, in the glare of the burning cruiser another appeared, apparently chasing the Stuart, who was busy shelling the victim of the heavy list. As if this was not crowding the moment with incident enough, an Italian destroyer shot past the Stuart, illuminated by a convenient explosion in one of the damaged cruisers. The Stuart, who had to dodge to port to avoid collision, put three salvoes into her as she swept past with the Havock in pursuit.

The Stuart, still swinging to port, now narrowly escaped collision with the cruiser Captain Waller of the Stuart previously thought to be chasing him. Apparently taking the Stuart for a friend, she ignored her, and Captain Waller, who had fired all his torpedoes, did nothing to disillusion her; instead he went off soft-footed to look for his earlier victim. She was on fire when he found her. A few salvoes produced nothing but explosions, and in his own words, " I considered her good enough to leave till morning." He had then lost touch with the Havock, and, as he puts it, " was feeling somewhat alone." This gallant unit of the Australian Navy then retired to the north-east and the cover of the Battle Fleet. On the way she engaged yet another cruiser and left her on fire.

We last saw the Havock disappearing in pursuit of a destroyer that the Stuart had severely mauled. Lieutenant G. R. G. Watkins, in command of the Havock, managed to get a torpedo into her, which brought her to a standstill. The Havock then circled her, pouring in a heavy fire until she blew up and sank.

It was now about 11.30 p.m. The Havock had lost touch with the Stuart, which

was retiring on the Battle Fleet. Passing through a number of rafts and survivors Lieutenant Watkins, who had by now released his remaining torpedoes, saw, by the light of a starshell, what he took to be yet another cruiser. This was the crippled Pola, bagged at dusk by the Fleet Air Arm. He fired a few rounds at her, which provoked no reply; she appeared undamaged, and in some bewilderment he ceased fire, hauled off and prepared a boarding party.

At this juncture the Greyhound and the Griffin appeared on the scene. The Pola, her ensign still flying, her guns trained fore and aft, was apparently undamaged. But a large number of her crew had unaccountably taken to the water, and the remainder, a disorganised rabble on the upper decks, were bawling surrender. The problem was whether to sink her, to carry her by boarding, or to go alongside and take the crew grateful prisoners. His consort, Lieutenant-Commander J. Lee Barber in the Griffin, was for boarding her with bayonet, cutlass and revolver. The Havock's captain had changed his mind about boarding and was preparing to blow the Pola's stern off with depth charges, having no torpedoes left.

Commander Marshall A'Deane was rescued from his quandary by the arrival of Captain Mack and the 14th and 2nd flotillas. They had failed to establish contact with the enemy fleet due to its timely " jig " to the southward, and now returned to the scene of the action, sinking the burning Zara on the way. Ordering his ships to pick survivors out of the water, Captain Mack took the Jervis alongside the Pola. Her upper deck was a scene of incredible demoralisation. Many of those who had not jumped overboard were half-drunk. The deck was littered with bottles, clothing, packages ; the guns were abandoned—indeed had not fired a shot.

By 3.40 a.m. this strange rescue work was completed. Casting off from the Pola, the Jervis put a torpedo into her. As she settled very slowly, the Nubian followed up with another. The Pola sank at 4.10 a.m. and the flotillas rejoined the Battle Fleet.

They were sighted from the bridge of the Fleet flagship as dawn was breaking, steaming in two divisions with the slightly self-conscious precision of a peace-time review. The Staff counted them through high-powered glasses. After the Witches' Sabbath through which they had passed, the report " There are all twelve there, Sir! " seemed to the anxious Commander-in-Chief almost incredible.

When, without stratagem,
But in plain shock and even play of battle,
Was ever known so great and little loss
On one part and on the other?

The previous afternoon, unknown to the Commander-in-Chief, a force of twenty-three Blenheim bombers from Greece had flown off, and having located the enemy Force Z, stopped one cruiser with two direct hits and a destroyer with one direct hit. A Greek flotilla of seven destroyers was also dispatched at once to join the British Commander-in-Chief, but arrived too late for the battle. This was a matter for regret, as their already proved gallantry would have undoubtedly cost the enemy further losses. As it was, the complete reckoning could not be assessed with accuracy. The fate of the Vittorio Veneto was uncertain. The Blenheims' bombs may have caused losses and the engagement between their own forces may have cost the enemy more. What is certain (" as per margin ") is that three 10,000-ton cruisers, the Pola, the Zara and the Fiume, and two 1,500-ton destroyers were sunk. The Captain of the Valiant's pet canary chose the height of the action to hatch out two of her eggs, and the resultant songsters are to-day named Pola and Zara.

Although the action was not a climax in the naval war, it had the effect of discouraging Italy from participating with her fleet in two vital operations which the future held, the withdrawal of the army from Greece, and the battle for Crete ; and as the record of the war unfolds it will be apparent how far-reaching were the effects of our Fleet's ascendancy during the earlier phases of the war in the Mediterranean which culminated in the Battle of Matapan.

THE CLIMAX AT MATAPAN. The British battleships crash their broadsides into the Italian cruisers which the destroyer Greyhound's searchlight has suddenly revealed. It was all over in less than two minutes: the Zara and the Fiume were set ablaze and later sunk. This painting by Lieut.-Cdr. Rowland Langmaid, R.N., shows, reading from left to right, the burning Zara and Fiume, the Barham, the Valiant and the flagship Warspite.

THE NAVY HOLDS THE NARROW SEAS

" It is upon the Navy, under the good providence of God, that the
wealth, safety and strength of the Kingdom do chiefly depend "